WORKING ON THE
RAILROAD

BRIAN SOLOMON

Voyageur
Press

WITHDRAWN

First published in 2006 by MBI Publishing Company and Voyageur Press, an imprint of MBI Publishing Company, Galtier Plaza, Suite 200, 380 Jackson Street, St. Paul, MN 55101-3885 USA

MBI Publishing Company titles are also available at discounts in bulk quantity for industrial or sales-promotional use. For details write to Special Sales Manager at MBI Publishing Company, Galtier Plaza, Suite 200, 380 Jackson Street, St. Paul, MN 55101-3885 USA

Library of Congress Cataloging–in-Publication Data

Solomon, Brian, 1966–
    Working on the Railroad / by Brian Solomon
        p. cm.
    ISBN-13: 978-0-7603-2220-8
    ISBN-10: 0-7603-2220-1
    1. Railroads—United States—History. 2. General Motors Corporation. Electo-Motive Division. I. Title.
    TF23.S66 2006
    385.0973—dc22

                                                    2006001499

Editor: Dennis Pernu
Designer: Kari Johnston

Printed in China

Front cover: Polish State Railways (PKP) still operates main line steam. On April 24, 2002, a crewmember carries lubrication equipment at the Wolsztyn roundhouse. *Brian Solomon*

Endpapers: On the evening of August 7, 1958, a Norfolk & Western fireman waits with Y6 Mallet No. 2129 at Boaz siding, east of Roanoke. N&W was an anomaly in mid-twentieth-century American railroading, resisting dieselization longer than any other main line carrier in the United States and designing and constructing its own locomotives until the mid-1950s. It finally dieselized in 1960, a full decade later than some other railroads. *Jim Shaughnessy*

Frontis: In a classic pose at Niagara Falls, Ontario, in February 1950, a senior engineer and a young fireman have just arrived from Toronto with Canadian National 4-8-2 No. 6062. *Jim Shaughnessy*

Title pages: A Soo Line conductor lines the switch back for the main line behind Soo caboose 227 west at Genoa, Illinois, in May 1991, as the crew prepares for a meet with an eastbound grain extra on the former Milwaukee Road main line between Bensenville and Savanna, Illinois. Advances in technology made the caboose redundant; they were largely phased out during the 1980s and early 1990s. *Steve Smedley*

Contents page: A searchlight signal is silhouetted on Shed 10 on Union Pacific's former Southern Pacific line over Donner Pass. *Brian Solomon*

Back cover, top: A trainman at the back of a Denver & Rio Grande Western freight on August 29, 1967. The Rio Grande's narrow gauge lines in Colorado and New Mexico operated in a time warp and maintained traditional operating methods until the lines were abandoned. *John Gruber*
Bottom: A Canadian Pacific conductor riding a coil car during a switching move in the Port of Milwaukee, Wisconsin, displays his loyalty to the Milwaukee Road, which was absorbed by CP affiliate Soo Line in 1985. *Patrick Yough*

CONTENTS

Acknowledgments...6

Foreword...8

Introduction: The Evolution of Railroad Work...16

1 Railroading 101: Brakemen...36

2 In Charge of the Train: The Conductor...52

3 At the Throttle: Engineers and Firemen...74

4 The Big Picture: Levermen, Operators, and Dispatchers...108

5 Working on the Railroad (Literally): Maintenance...138

Glossary...154

Bibliography...158

Index...160

ACKNOWLEDGMENTS

My cumulative railroading knowledge comes from spending time with innumerable railroaders over the years, each of whom helped my understanding of railroad operations through their explanations and demonstrations. I hope to use this knowledge to help decipher the principles and details of railroad operations and the jobs that railroaders perform.

ALTHOUGH the principles behind railroad technologies are often relatively simple, their applications are complex and sometimes counterintuitive. Railroad rules and their evolution, differences, and application are the subjects of detailed study by railroaders everywhere. These rules are necessary to ensure efficient, coordinated, and, above all, safe operations. Today railroading has an excellent safety record—much better than that of highway transport—but trains are always potentially dangerous and individual mistakes are fatal. The safety culture of modern railroading ensures that accidents are rare events. When every train departs, railroaders wish it and its crew a "safe trip," and although opinions differ on how to make each trip as safe as possible, every railroader has safety in his or her best interest. I've learned crucial aspects of railroad safety from every railroader I've ever met.

During the year that this book was in production, I conducted roughly three dozen formal interviews and dozens more informal discussions. These interviews and talks were necessary to help me better understand the railroads that I've studied in detail for years. Thanks to everyone who participated, including: Jim Beagle; George W. Kowanski; Greg Cruickshank; Jay Grumblatt; Henry Kitchen; Travis Berryman; James J. Emerson; Pioneer Valley's Larry Runyon, Charlie O'Connell, Al Massey, and Joe Albano Jr.; Delaware-Lackawanna's Richard Janesko, Shawn Palermo, Ken Lucas, and Dave Heller; Cal-Northern's Tim Holbrook and Mark French; and dozens of active and retired employees of Amtrak, Boston & Maine, Burlington Northern Santa Fe, Canadian National, Canadian Pacific, Cape Breton & Central Nova Scotia, Central Vermont, Chicago & North Western, Chicago Metra, Conrail, CSX, Iarnród Éireann, Iowa, Chicago & Eastern, Louisiana & Delta, New England Central, Norfolk Southern, Santa Fe, Southern Pacific, Susquehanna, Union Pacific, Wisconsin Central, and Wisconsin & Southern.

Special thanks to Doug Riddell for his detailed explanations, personal introductions, hospitality, and writings. Not only is Doug a respected professional railroader, but he has the rare ability to clarify the details of his occupation with wit, humor, clarity, and style. Thanks to my old friend Dave Swirk of the Pioneer Valley Railroad for unrestricted access and answers to my multitude of questions, covering everything from track maintenance to the repair of 567 engines. Doug Eisele, another old friend, made trips on the Delaware-Lackawanna possible. Chris Goeple of the California Northern made access possible on that line. Tom Carver of the Adirondack Scenic was extraordinarily generous and provided many answers on operations and details of locomotive performance. Marshall Beecher and Mike Abalos hosted tours in greater Chicago. Dick Gruber opened doors on Wisconsin & Southern and detailed track maintenance procedure. Over the years, I've sat in on many dispatching sessions and enjoyed the view from numerous signal towers. Thanks to each and every operator, signal-man, leverman, tower director, and dispatcher for answering my constant questions on railroad signaling. Thanks to George S. Pitarys for lending me examples of train orders and explaining the details of the delivery process. And thanks to Ed King for his dispatcher sidebar.

In addition to my own photography, I've borrowed images from a variety of excellent photographers and each one is credited appropriately. Special thanks go to Jim Shaughnessy and William D. Middleton for their histori-cal images. John Gruber's help with this project has been extensive and invaluable. His own excellent photography, his tireless efforts promoting railroad photography, and his skill in seeking out information, people, and railroad stories have been works of passion. Thanks, too, for his contributions to this text.

Patrick Yough provided great help in many ways: he made introductions, gave me access to his library, answered signaling questions, assisted with interviews, provided photographs, and made photographs especially for this book. In addition, he also helped with captions and text proofing. Tim Doherty aided with intellectual discussion and photographic issues. Brian Jennison provided wit and comment. T. S. Hoover assisted with technical inquiries. The Irish Railway Record Society in Dublin gave me unre-stricted access to their facilities, and years ago when I worked at Pentrex, Sean Graham-White arranged a detailed tour of Belt Railway of Chicago's Clearing Yard.

My father, Richard Jay Solomon, introduced me to railroads and took me on my first visits to signal towers and on early train rides. He also loaned me the use of his library and darkroom, and assisted with proofing. My mother, Maureen, helped in many ways as well, including by providing needed office support.

Finally, without the labor of Dennis Pernu and every-one at MBI Publishing Company, all of this effort would have yielded little more than a file folder full of computer printouts and a stack of images—their work has trans-formed my work into this book. Enjoy!

—*Brian Solomon*
Dublin, Ireland

FOREWORD

John Gruber, President
Center for Railroad Photography & Art

THE ORIGINS of the tune are cloudy. Some believe it is a "Louisiana levee" song of African Americans, while others claim it is an old hymn adapted by the Irish work gangs in the West. Most think of "I've Been Working on the Railroad" as a lighthearted folk song. In truth, there is nothing quaint or lighthearted about railroad work. Railroad people are on the road at all times of the day and night. It has been that way from the beginning, and while today there are far fewer railroad employees, the work goes on 24/7.

Modern railroading in the United States is in many ways a last frontier where some work outside in all kinds of weather, while others spend their entire shift sitting in front of computer screens. The railroad is like no other employer. A worker's life is defined by demanding work rules, irregular hours of service, and a host of labor, safety, and retirement laws that set railroading apart from other industries. Even the U.S. Supreme Court, in a 1957 decision (*Taylor vs. California*), observed that "the railroad world is like a state within a state."

In many ways, the nature of the work sets railroaders, not just the industry, a world apart. For generations, jobs have been passed from fathers to sons and now to daughters as well. Family connections, experiences with your dad or brother, can provide insight to the realities of railroad life. Take a look at the Cain family in Illinois or the Burringtons in Montana or the Shipleys in Wisconsin.

"The Cain family knows a good thing when they find it. My father was a railroader, I was a railroader, and my son is a railroader," says Leland "Sugar" Cain, who retired in 1996 after 53 years as a chef-cook for the Chicago & North Western and Chicago's Regional Transit Authority. "I had a daughter who was a railroader, and she was in the yards. Working for the railroad was the best thing that ever happened to my family."

At one period in the 1960s, three generations of Burringtons worked at the same time out of Harlowton, Montana. Alex Cox and his son, Curren Daniel Burrington, both worked as engineers on the Milwaukee Road. Dan's son, Lee Burrington, worked as a brakeman during the summer breaks in high school and college. Dan found that the railroad paid better than his father's ranch. "At that time, to show you the difference, eight hours on the switch engine in the yard paid $6.07 per day in '41. When I left [in 1978] we were making around $70 on an eight-hour day. There's quite a difference. Over the years, with union help, we got those things improved."

The Shipleys of the Milwaukee Road counted 250 years of cumulative service. Willard, a conductor, worked for more than 50 years. His father, Frank, was an agent at Cross Plains, Wisconsin, for 57 years. His brother Frank Jr. retired as a trainman after 42 years, brother Jay was an engineer for 54 years, and brother Robert retired after more than 48 years as chief yard clerk in Tacoma, Washington.

On the Western Maryland railroad, nine Rhodes brothers all hired out as locomotive engineers. Their feat made national headlines, including *Ripley's Believe It or Not* in 1952, but usually railroad family ties are noted quietly.

Continued on page 12

Milwaukee Road's Tom Farence at the throttle of a four-motor General Electric U-boat on December 28, 1980. John Gruber

Westward train No. 25, the *North Coast Limited*, is shown during its servicing stop at Billings, Montana, on July 31, 1969. Its toilets will be drained, water tanks refilled, and supplies restocked.
William D. Middleton

REMEMBERING WORK ON THE GREEN BAY & WESTERN

By John Gruber

Green Bay & Western, a Wisconsin institution from 1866 to 1993, is remembered for its dedication to traditional railroading: dependable freight service, self-contained repair shops, Alco locomotives, financial structure, well-maintained property, and, most of all, family traditions. For years in freight train ads, GB&W stressed the advantages of "the fast straightway route between east and west." A 1953 directory of industries showed a Howard Fogg painting of the Alco PA-1 freight diesels.

Passenger service declined after the automobile appeared, and a mixed train quietly replaced the passenger train in 1934. Suggestions, never implemented, included a *Hiawatha*-like streamlined 4-4-2 steam locomotive (Alco drawing, 1936) and a *Zephyr*-like lightweight diesel train (1935).

The GB&W continued the in-house repair tradition common to the steam era, but it was unusual in the 1990s. Originally built for the small engines that were typical at the beginning of the twentieth century, with only minor modifications the shops were later used for larger steam locomotives and diesels (all Alco since 1907). If something broke or wore out on the GB&W, "We just fixed it," personnel said. It was a self-contained industrial complex, with well-maintained air and wheel shops. It did all its locomotive maintenance, except for main generators and traction motors—which was rare even then.

The family names Schultz, Pronschinske, Sansalla, Beyer, and many others are a part of GB&W history. The railroad encouraged hiring from its "family."

"The father would have good success on the railroad, and he would encourage his son or sons to work on the railroad. It was a compliment. Unlike some companies, the GB&W never had a policy against hiring family members," said H. Weldon McGee, who went to work for the GB&W in 1935. He succeeded his father as president in 1962, serving until 1978 when Itel purchased the company.

"If a son of one of our employees wanted to work for us, we assumed that he knew a little bit about the conditions," McGee continued. "If, after hearing conversations at home, [he] would think the railroad was a good place to work, we'd know he would accept some of the bitter with the sweet.

"When you are devoted to the railroad, you have to accept some difficult working conditions. I certainly did years ago. You know you are going to be called out at hours when you don't really want to go. Sons would learn that from their fathers; if you didn't like that way of life, then don't go into railroading."

During World War II when the railroad added a women's track crew, many came from the family

Roger Sansalla repairs Green Bay & Western track at sunset on June 21, 1993. A very efficient crew was at work to repair a washout from a flood on the Trempealeau River. *John Gruber*

ranks. Of 137 hourly employees on the summer 1993 payroll, 45 had a father, son, or brother who was also working for the GB&W.

The GB&W had expected its sale to be effective before 1993. But while the Fox Valley & Western, a Wisconsin Central Ltd. subsidiary, negotiated implementing agreements with six labor unions, business remained strong. The line shut down in the early morning hours of August 28, 1993, and FV&W took over. Today, what's left of the GB&W is a part of Canadian National.

"The people really make the railroad," said Jerold J. Bruley, a former president of the GB&W who retired in 1991 after 37 years of service. His son still works for CN. "The locomotives and buildings, bridges, offices, and shops are needed to operate a railroad, but all of those things are immaterial and they really mean very little until you put people in them, and you have an organization that works together like a team."

Looking back, in 2005, Bruley added, "We might not have been the biggest in the state, but we were the best in caring for the customers. We got

the job done real fine. You only get back what you put into it. We tried to be a good carrier for all of our connections and our people and our customers, and also to the public."

Bruley's pride in railroading and the GB&W resulted in a photographic record of the final years of the central Wisconsin short line. It connected Lake Michigan and the Mississippi River through central Wisconsin in 1873. Bruley introduced me to employees all along the route and made these photographs possible. They are a tribute to the people who kept the railroad going in all kinds of weather. Enjoy this unusual glimpse of traditional railroading—it's a tribute to all the employees who, through the years, have contributed so much to our rich railroad heritage.

⋒ Fred Loften and Tim Burke assist passengers on Milwaukee Road No. 22 on the run from Madison to Chicago. Passenger service employees needed to maintain courtesy and decorum at all times. John Gruber

⮑ Milwaukee Road train No. 22 makes its last station stop at Madison, Wisconsin, on April 30, 1971, one day before Amtrak came into being and ended regular passenger service to Madison. Trainman Tim Burke helps passengers board the train. John Gruber

Continued from page 8

Railroad companies encouraged a family approach or perspective with articles in their company magazines. The Norfolk & Western showed the six Spangler brothers on the cover of its February 1950 magazine.

Even today, an informal count shows four pairs of fathers/daughters or sons, plus two pairs of brothers and a nephew, employed in 2005 by the Wisconsin & Southern, a regional line that operates 645 miles of track in south central Wisconsin and northern Illinois.

Religion and ethnicity also played a role in railroaders' identities and in some instances it dictated their occupational possibilities. "You had to be Catholic to get on the Milwaukee Road," says a retired yardmaster-switchman. At one time, just about everyone working the Milwaukee Road was Irish-American.

Railroaders have a language all their own. A brakeman "reaching in to make the joint" is talking about pulling a car out of a siding, not about getting high. W. Fred Cottrell, who in 1940 wrote *The Railroaders*, one of the few studies of railroad work, said "language is a tag which makes it easy to distinguish those who do from those who

do not" work for the railroad. However, this railroad vernacular is fading.

As a working team and extended family, railroaders have also taken care of one another. They have had to do so, especially when far away from headquarters. When a dining car worker named "Whiskey Sim" missed the *Dakota 400* in Huron, South Dakota, the dispatcher stopped the train 40 miles out of town and local railroaders sent him on a switch engine to catch up with the train. There are many such stories, although even today railroaders will not talk about most of them publicly.

Railroad towns have also had their own unique flavor. The Chicago & Alton shops dominated Bloomington, Illinois, for many decades, but all that is gone now. The tradition, however, survives in a few towns like Glendive, Montana, where the railroad remains its economic lifeblood. Glendive is still an active stopover point for freight trains to change crews. Here, railroaders raise their families and actively participate in the civic life of their community.

The railroad industry has typically remained steeped in tradition and resistant to social or economic change. Yet, significant changes in race relations have occurred in the industry. In 1918, the United States Railroad Administration's director general of railroads pioneered for all U.S. industrial relations. National rates of pay would be the same for the same class of rail service without regard to sex or race. While there were limitations in practice, it was an important symbolic mandate and a starting point.

Unions also promoted social and economic changes. The Joint Council of Dining Car Employees, which was organized in 1937 and represented 15 locals, negotiated wage increases as well as a historic 1961 declaration adopted by the Railway Labor Executives Association for "equal rights for all workers in the railroad industry." The Brotherhood of Sleeping Car Porters was a notable agent of change—it provided the support necessary to organize Martin Luther King Jr.'s march on Washington in 1963.

Just as social climates change, so do the technologies used to run trains and schedule them. "The railroad has changed quite a bit," says Tom Farence, who was a railroader from 1967 to 2005. "Today the whole system works off radios. More technology is involved, with caboose-less operations, and more structure. Years ago, there was cushion; today, there is more federal regulation."

There still are freight pools. "Everything is based on two hours calls; crews have to be ready to go," Farence explains. "You can't have a quality life and make big money. Our railroad tried to set up a lot more structure, so guys knew when they were going to work, but that resulted in a lower pay scale."

Interestingly, not many publications have investigated the historical and contemporary cultures of railroad work.

For much of the period of industrialization in the United States, railroads were the single largest non-farm employer in this country. In 1920, for example, more than 2.2 million people worked for railways. According to the U.S. Census, railroaders accounted for 7.25 percent of the labor force in 1920. Yet, the 68,942 locomotives in service that year have received far more attention. By 1960, the number of employees was down to 883,000.

While railroad employment numbers in the twenty-first century have continued to drop dramatically (to 227,000 in 2004) from those of earlier times, railroaders continue to perform their duties in the time-honored railroad manner that is dominated by the demands of flanged wheel on steel rail technology. As in the past, many feel the pressure to put their work before everything else in their lives. In many ways, the industry is busier and more efficient than ever before, but it's still a world apart from most other industries.

The Center for Railroad Photography & Art in Madison, Wisconsin, is bringing a human face to railroading. Its three-year project, funded by the North American Railway Foundation, "Representations of Railroad Work, Past and Present," wraps up its first phase in September 2006, with more initiatives in the works. "The human element of railroading, the focus of our project, often is ignored or minimized. Railroads are some of the earliest examples of modern corporations. The workers who built these organizations, rail by rail, have a very important, often overlooked story to tell," the center reports. It has produced six exhibits on the theme of railroad work, both historical and contemporary.

So enjoy the insights provided by Brian Solomon, with the knowledge that you are getting a glimpse into the lives of a unique set of hardworking people.

◖ Doug Hanson spent most of his working years in Chicago & North Western stations in small Wisconsin communities, starting in 1949. When photographed handling two phones, he was an agent at Baraboo, one of the last open agencies in the Badger State. He continued there for another year, and then sold commuter tickets at Woodstock and Cary, Illinois, until retiring in 1989. John Gruber

COMPANY PHOTOGRAPHER

By John Gruber

The company photographer disappeared years ago on the main line railroads, but the job is still alive on the commuter lines in the New York City area.

Frank English, who has worked for Metro-North's corporate and media relations department since 1984, is an example of a company photographer, and an amazing one at that. He thrives on informal employee portraits and retirement parties—assignments that would send other photographers quickly hunting for new employment—while successfully making the transition to a "new way" of seeing images digitally.

English's main venue is the monthly employee magazine, *On Track*. "For me, it's a family album. These people are hard working, unrecognized, and even if they don't read it, they love to look at their pictures," explains English. "They come up to me all the time, and say, 'I didn't see myself in there. Come on, take my picture.' That's my favorite feedback. It is nice to make a nice graphic statement, but to me it is more important that people feel like this revealed something of them, without trying to make it dark like Irving Penn or Sebastião Solgado. These are people who want to bring the magazine home and show their children, so they want to be smiling and proud. Maybe that is corny, and I guess it is in a way, but if I can express what they do and the strength and intelligence that they bring to it, that is the most important thing."

He talks about how his photograph of three smiling workers showing off their new uniforms in Grand Central illustrates teamwork on the railroad. "They are aware of each other's strengths and histories and so, if I am posing them, I want to show something that will last. You look at it 10 years from

now and one of them might have died, it'll still hang together. It'll still look like it was made just to illustrate that story.

"Since it is an employee paper, most of the stories, even if they are technical, I try to illustrate from the employee's point of view. If you want people to read it, for that reason alone, you want to do it. But I find when I pose them together, I will be straightening their ties, putting the hat brim back far enough so the shadow will not be over their eyes, getting the dandruff off. Everybody is embarrassed to get his or her picture taken, almost everybody. They still look kind of distant even if they are standing next to one another, so I will relax them for a bit, waste some film, talk with them, so finally it is like they are not worrying about the camera working. I have already clicked it enough they are no longer paying attention. Then I will start saying something like, 'You know, if you just put you arm a little over here,' and these people maybe would not be touching one another. And suddenly they are totally relaxed, because they really do work that closely. And then I will go over to the other side, move another hand over, 'Let's do it this way so the pin on your lapel looks okay,' whatever reason you give them. Pretty soon there is another chemistry going which reflects their psychology, the way they work together, and the image they present as a unit working with customers or with internal customers, because the 5,500 people on the team have to work with each other.

"So I think of it that way. It's not just a way of pulling the people together so the portrait will look good formally. I do like it to have a good shape. I want this line to go out of the frame at this angle, and at that angle. That is like a building block. Then you use those building blocks as a way of extracting from the people some central thing about them."

Surrounded by music speakers, English continues to talk about his photographic experiences at the railroad. He is proud of the retirement photos and shows people he has worked with. "It comes time to retire, they bring their children, their grandchildren, everybody comes in. They are so proud of this man who has given his whole life to it, and I get to document the family. That to me is interesting. That is like being an anthropologist going to the Amazon, except the Amazon comes to me."

When Lenny Maglione retired as general superintendent of the terminal, people who had been retired for 10 to 20 years came back. "Many, many people came together, and since I have known all these people for 20 years, that kind of thing to me is exciting."

English was pleased to attend the retirement for Roger Nichols, an employee who could fix anything. "The guy was just astonishing. I think they were wondering what would happen when he retired. He did manage to find a young guy who he trained for about three years, who had the natural talent, who also could fix anything. We have a place called the heavy repair shop, and there are cars that people would say never can be repaired, or would have to be sent to the manufacturer. We [would] send the car up to [Nichols'] heavy repair shop, and if the parts did not exist, he could machine the parts for it."

Without Nichols and a hockey puck, the Cos Cob power plant on the New Haven line would have been out of service for a Monday morning commuter rush. The power plant, providing a kind of power that Metro-North couldn't buy from anybody, broke down over the weekend. English recalls, "How are we going to fix it? The part does not exist. Roger came in, and he cut the right part out of a hockey puck that had the right dielectric properties, and was the right size, and the right strength. So this entire power plant was running Monday morning

because Roger could figure out what to do with the hockey puck. The railroad is filled with stories like that, so when a retirement comes, all the people who have worked together come in and reminisce. I don't just stay there to get the group shots. I stay there and get everything, all the old stories. To me, that's exciting."

Metro-North staff photographer Frank English takes a portrait of paint shop foreman Will Clark in front of New York Central–painted FL9 No. 2013 at North White Plains, New York, in 1999. *Patrick Yough*

INTRODUCTION

THE EVOLUTION OF RAILROAD WORK

DURING THE nineteenth century, American railroads evolved as a complex, privately owned transportation network extending to all corners of the nation. Along with this network, a specialized labor force was formed to coordinate, operate, service, and maintain the trains, tracks, equipment, and infrastructure. A host of different and defined crafts were born to carry out day-to-day operations. By the end of the nineteenth century, American railroads employed an army of men (and some women) who were skilled in the details of keeping it running. By 1929, the count of laborers had grown to approximately 1.6 million people.

Inherent technological constraints contributed to the railroad's need for specialized skilled labor. The inflexibility of the basic track structure, combined with dynamic difficulties in both propelling and keeping heavy vehicles under control, have made running a railroad a unique proposition. Coordinating the myriad jobs performed by thousands of people over hundreds of miles of track resulted in the development of a distinctive command and control structure, while specific job crafts evolved to fulfill the various needs of railroad operations.

Operational practices developed during the formative years of the American railroads in the middle part of the nineteenth century as technology matured. Numerous small railroads gradually coalesced from short point-to-point operations into large integrated systems that set the norms for various crafts and procedures. By the dawn of the twentieth century, most American railroads had adopted similar labor practices, although minor differences remained that often characterized specific operations.

Railroads largely employed a method of command and control that mimicked a military model. Employees such as locomotive engineers, brakemen, and telegraph operators engauged in hands-on operations may be compared to enlisted men, while the hands-on managers, such as trainmasters and superintendents, are equivalent to officers.

Beginning in 1863 with the formation of the Brotherhood of Locomotive Engineers, most railroad craftsmen joined specialized trade unions. Eventually, operational employees worked under agreements that were made between their unions and railroad managements. Richard Saunders Jr., in his book *Merging Lines*, points out that the division of craft unions, whereby each craft had individual representation, "was peculiar to railroads." The craft divisions remained in railroad work throughout the twentieth century and added to the character, complexity, and individuality of railroad work. This characteristic also made labor negotiation and changes to the nature of the work force and to job descriptions more challenging than in other industries.

An Amtrak conductor speaks into his handheld train radio to advise his engineer during a back-up move at New Haven, Connecticut, on November 23, 1988. Brian Solomon

After years of hard work as a
brakeman, and possibly as a
freight conductor, a man with
enough seniority might be able
to bid for a job as a passenger
conductor. A Boston & Maine
conductor waits for passengers
on the platform at Bellows Falls,
Vermont, in October 1964.
Richard Jay Solomon

BY THE RULES

A railroad's vast labor force is comprised of various interacting crafts that often lack direct supervision. Due to the railroad's nature, clearly defined rules are necessary. Almost every aspect of railroad operation is governed by rules using very specific language to dictate procedure. A railroader's actions are governed by the company rulebook from the time he hires on until he earns his last paycheck. The rules have evolved to reflect changes in the industry, but without the rules, railroads would be incapable of orderly safe operation.

Old Nickel Plate Road No. 759 gets a wipe-down between excursion trips at Delaware & Hudson's Mohawk Yard near Schenectady, New York. Jim Shaughnessy

TRACKS, TRAINS, AND MEN

The basic nature of a railroad is its use of fixed tracks that support and guide trains over a low friction roadway. These tracks require minimal real estate to haul very heavy loads and just a few people do a job that once required many. On the negative side, a railroad track does not allow operational flexibility. In order for trains to pass or overtake one another, passing tracks must be provided. Passing tracks can only be accessed by switches at pre-established locations. In addition, the low friction between steel wheels and steel rails, combined with the enormous weight of trains, results in very long stopping distances that typically extend beyond the locomotive engineer's line of sight.

To ensure safety, railroads must maintain a system that does not allow trains to physically get in one another's way. Track occupancy must be carefully allocated and the speeds and stopping points of trains must be strictly governed so that operators have sufficient notice to keep their trains under control and can operate in a safe yet efficient manner. In some situations, trains are operated at slow speeds so that they can be brought to a safe stop within sight limits. Since a train may be approaching from the opposite direction, this concept means engineers must be able to stop within one half of their sight limits. This basic system is the essence behind the concept of "restricted speed," which many railroads use within their yards, on passing sidings, or in other places where elaborate and expensive control systems are deemed unnecessary or not cost effective.

It is neither practical nor desirable to keep trains moving at restricted speeds in most situations, thus some control of track occupancy is required. Over the years, a variety of different control systems have been developed. The telegraph was the first major innovation. Later, automatic block signals, Centralized Traffic Control, the telephone, and finally radio came to play important roles in the safe movement of trains.

On January 15, 1993, Southern Pacific mainte-nance-of-way forces clear snow from the line at Truckee, California. SP's route over Donner Pass received some of the heaviest snowfall anywhere in North America. Brian Solomon

IMPROVING PRODUCTIVITY

In the nineteenth century, the telegraph allowed railroads to increase track capacity and improved the timely movement of trains. In addition, the development of the Bessemer steel process resulted in comparatively inexpensive steel for stronger and less brittle rails. The new steel process also facilitated the development of larger and more powerful locomotives. Larger locomotives and heavier rails allowed railroads to move larger and faster trains. As a result, the labor force's productivity effectively increased. As train size grew, a single train crew could haul more goods. With the increasing train size, railroads needed to upgrade their infrastructures to accommodate the bigger, heavier, and faster trains. Old routes laid out in the formative days of railroading were straightened, grades were eased, and bridges improved. Steel construction permitted better and larger bridges at lower cost.

In the early days, when trains had operated infrequently with short consists and at relatively slow speeds, accidents were uncommon and generally not very serious. With the frantic pace of the mid-nineteenth-century railroad development, competition for traffic became fierce as the size and speed of trains grew by leaps and bounds. Safety was too often overlooked. By the mid-1870s, railroad accidents had become commonplace and serious collisions occurred on a weekly basis. While accidents involving passenger trains made big headlines and outraged the public, even run-of-the-mill railroading had become hazardous. Most fatalities were employees killed on the job. During this wild and dangerous time, thousands of railroaders lost their lives every year, and many more were injured and maimed.

The perceived attitude of railroad management toward safety did little to endear them to the public or the rank-and-file employees. It was never the intent of the railroads, their employees, or their management to establish dangerous working practices. However, management's goal of running railroads efficiently, keeping trains on time, and moving as much freight as possible often conflicted with safety. While railroad rules were designed to maintain safe operating practices, sometimes rules were bent, safe practices were ignored, and reasonable speeds were exceeded. A poorly trained railroader, out of ignorance or neglect, could have made an error. Experienced railroaders also made mistakes. In the raw, old-fashioned 1800s, railroading was unforgiving with errors.

Getting a train to move has always been the easier task in railroading. Stopping trains—or the failure to stop them—too often results in accidents. The engineer of a late-running passenger train who is racing to make up time may fail to yield to a stop signal, or in haste miss the signal altogether. An experienced crew with a heavy freight descending a mountain too quickly may meet their doom at the bottom of a ravine if the train runs out of control. In the gloom of a rainy night, a brakeman may be flattened in a yard by his own crew because a cut of cars moves at the wrong time—just when the brakeman least expects it. A local freight may misinterpret a timetable or train order, overrun its track authority, and run afoul of a passenger train. In each situation, the inability to stop at the correct moment leads to an accident. There are other causes of accidents, to be sure, but the inherent difficulty of stopping trains has long been the bane of operations. As long as trains are moving, the potential for accident exists.

Ultimately, state and federal governments forced railroads to adopt safer operating procedures and better work practices. As a result of these regulations, a safer industry prevailed. Since the later years of the nineteenth century, maintaining safety and obtaining greater productivity have been continuing themes in the evolution of American railroads and railroad labor practices.

All employees were encouraged to observe passing trains. A westward Nickel Plate Road freight approaches a grade-crossing shanty at North East, Pennsylvania, on St. Patrick's Day, 1957, as a crossing guard protects the crossing and observes the train. Today, talking defect detectors check for abnormal conditions while flashers and automatic gates protect the crossings. Jim Shaughnessy

SAFER, FASTER AND BIGGER RAILROADING

One of railroading's most important technological safety and productivity innovations was the development of the Westinghouse automatic air brake in 1873. However, railroads were slow to embrace it because of the great cost involved to apply air-brake equipment to vast fleets of railroad cars and locomotives. The federal government ultimately forced the issue by making air brakes compulsory for passenger trains, and later for freight. Railroads benefited by being able to operate much longer freight trains (and substantially faster passenger trains) while requiring fewer brakemen per train. The addition of air brakes changed the nature of railroad operations and improved productivity.

After 1900, railroads were forced to adopt steel-framed and later steel-bodied railway cars, both to reduce fire hazards and to strengthen car bodies. Cars became much stronger but also substantially heavier, and required more powerful locomotives to move the heavier trains.

Additionally, advances in automatic signaling increased track capacity while maintaining or improving safety. Automatic signaling minimized the need for additional signal operators and was among the early instances of technology being used to supplant people in the railroad industry.

A man protects a highway grade crossing at a Middle-town, New York, yard as an NW2 switches with a wooden caboose on March 23, 1957. Jim Shaughnessy

A mechanic cleans the windshield of New York, Ontario & Western F3 No. 502 on March 23, 1957, shortly before the railroad ceased operations. The NYO&W was one of the first larger railroads to succumb to financial insolvency. Efforts to keep the line going by using diesel power and installing Centralized Traffic Control failed. Jim Shaughnessy

THE TWENTIETH-CENTURY METAMORPHOSIS

The railway changed the world in the nineteenth century, but in the twentieth century the world changed the railway. Nowhere was this more evident than in the United States. American railroads transformed and dominated transportation in the 1800s and railroaders were idolized as modern heroes. In the 1900s, events external to the railroad diminished its importance, dashed its preeminence, and forced it to implement widespread changes in its operations. Some of the greatest changes occurred with the labor force. During the twentieth century, the railroad moved from one of the nation's foremost employers to a relatively minor one. Many long-established crafts were combined or phased out and eliminated entirely. These shifts were painful and disruptive to railroaders who endured dramatic upheaval as their professions evolved or dissolved.

One of the greatest transitions to affect the roles of the railroad and its workers was the gradual dominance of petroleum-based transport. During the twentieth century, public highways became the dominant national transport network. Ever-growing competition from cars and trucks eroded whole aspects of railroad traffic. Where railroads were once the dominant form of transportation—carrying people and freight of all descriptions—advances in highway transport relegated the railroads to more specialized tasks. Most prominent for the public was the loss of passenger traffic. By the 1970s, passenger traffic was reduced to a fraction of the business once carried. The remaining intercity routes were run by the federally sponsored Amtrak, and suburban lines moved to local and state commuter agencies. Postal and express package traffic, formerly an integral part of the passenger business, also largely vanished. Railroads lost many of their smaller customers and exited the less-than-carload business. Traditional regional staples, such as fresh milk traffic in the Northeast, were entirely lost to the highway. The shift from coal to oil as a home-heating fuel helped doom anthracite-hauling lines such as the Delaware, Lackawanna & Western and the New York, Ontario & Western; the former merged with its competitor Erie Railroad in 1960, the latter was liquidated and abandoned in 1957 after a long

bankruptcy. By the 1980s, many railroads focused their efforts on moving bulk traffic in the form of coal, grain, ore, timber, and transcontinental intermodal shipments. While they continued to move a variety of other traffic, they had ceased to function effectively as common carriers.

The loss of traditional traffic contributed to the loss of railroad work and the phasing out of whole crafts that were once vital to the industry. The small-town station agent mostly vanished. Likewise, the freight agent largely disappeared.

Another crucial twentieth century change was the great increase in the cost of labor following World War I. While this affected all industries, it hit railroads especially hard. In the 1800s, when labor was inexpensive and immigration ensured a constant fresh supply of laborers, railroads could hire armies of people to operate and repair locomotives, turn down brakes, keep signal lamps filled with oil, protect grade crossings, and apply decorative paint to stations, passenger cars, and just about anything else. The cost of the individual employee to the railroad was little more than his daily wage. Gradually, these costs became more burdensome as wages rose and "extras" such as health benefits, pensions, and paid vacations became the norm or were required by law.

Railroads operated in fixed territories and were largely unable to relocate facilities in pursuit of less expensive labor, as other industries did. Furthermore, many railroads served regions that suffered from the loss of traditional businesses that had moved on. Railroads were also at a disadvantage for serving many new businesses that had been built around highway transport. Railroad infrastructure had been put in place with the advantage of low-cost nineteenth-century labor. It was much more difficult to build new lines in the twentieth century with higher labor and materials costs, and the competition of government-sponsored highways. With few exceptions, the vast majority of American railroads were privately financed and built prior to 1910.

In the nineteenth century, railroads were largely free to grow and prosper strictly in response to raw capitalist market realities. By doing so, they often shaped industrial and economic growth around them. During the early decades of the twentieth century, however, American railroads came under the increasingly heavy yoke of government regulation. In part, it was a delayed response to real and perceived abuses by the railroad companies of earlier eras. Regulation produced a variety of changes. It

railroads to invest in expensive equipment, such as air brakes and modern signaling, and it helped establish a safety culture among railroaders. Regulation also cemented railroad labor practices in an effort to quell the devastating social and economic effects of strikes. And, on antitrust grounds, it disrupted railroad plans for consolidation and merger.

Another federal action that had profound and long-lasting effects on American railroads was the temporary nationalization of American railroad operations between 1917 and 1920, coinciding with American involvement in World War I. During this period, railroads were operated under the United States Railroad Administration. Although the railroads were eventually returned to private ownership, the fear of renewed government control and re-nationalization of railroad operations cast a pall on the way railroads conducted their business, merger plans, and labor relations for the rest of the century. Any hint of government interference, imposition, or control was met with resentment and hostility. For the most part, railroads were opposed to any form of government subsidy for less-than-profitable services. Not until the 1970s, when the industry appeared to be on the brink of an abyss, did some railroads acquiesce to government aid—and then only reluctantly. By that time, several major lines had fallen into financial ruin

🔊 A Northern Pacific shopman at St. Paul, Minnesota, modifies a streamlined passenger car truck for the application of modern disc brakes on April 7, 1959. William D. Middleton

set up strict and complex rate structures that limited the amount railroads could charge for their services. It limited the railroads' abilities to introduce, discontinue, and curtail services. It set safety standards, which compelled

Norfolk Southern coal trains are lined up and await departure at South Roanoke, Virginia, on June 30, 2000, as a mechanic makes a minor repair to a lead unit. T. S. Hoover

Metro-North yardmaster Taras Olesnyckyj multitasks by applying blue light and derail protection at the Harmon Shop while speaking to the Fleet Management Office regarding the whereabouts of a car. Patrick Yough

Metro-North bridge electricians disconnect wires on the Saga Bridge on the former New Haven Railroad at Westport, Connecticut, on October 25, 2003. Pat Yough

Berlin, Connecticut, station agent Bill Semple assists a regular passenger with his tickets and gives him Amtrak's latest national timetable on October 11, 2005.
Brian Solomon

NEW TECHNOLOGY

The modern history of American railway labor practices stems from equating improved productivity with progress: fewer people to do more work. Pressure from growing competition and the inability to adjust their business model in other ways forced American railroads to aim for increased productivity through advancement of new technology. This had to be done within the constraints of the safety culture demanding safe operations with respect to progress.

The most obvious and dramatic technological change was the implementation of diesel-electric locomotive traction between 1925 and 1960. Briefly, diesel-electric locomotives offered railroads a more efficient and cost-effective method of moving trains. Diesels cost far less both to operate and maintain than steam engines, and they gave railroads great pulling power and superior braking ability under a throttle in control of a single engineer. With diesels, railroads were able to haul more freight with fewer crews. Furthermore, since diesels required less maintenance and repair, they allowed railroads to vastly scale back shop forces. Since diesels could move more freight, had greater availability, and traveled farther than steam locomotives between servicing stops, railroads needed fewer locomotives—and fewer people to work on them and run them.

Diesels brought other changes, too. First, diesels are bi-directional and have little need for turning facilities. Since basic servicing only requires fuel, sand, and water, many small roundhouses that were used to store and maintain steam engines could be closed. Second, diesels use standardized parts that are generally purchased directly from the manufacturer. The diesel's versatility eliminated much of the need for heavy shop forces that custom built components for steam locomotives. Third, superior starting ability eliminated the need for numerous helper districts all around the country. Where trains once stopped to cut in a pusher, they could now roll right through as the engineer notched back the throttle from "run 5" to "run 8" to conquer a grade.

Other technology included the gradual implementation of Centralized Traffic Control signaling that eliminated the need for countless trackside operator stations and towers, and opened ever larger and more distant centralized dispatching centers. The use of the two-way radio contributed to the reduction of crew size and ultimately the elimination of the caboose on most runs. The two-way radio also phased out the timetable and train-order system of train dispatching. The development of electronic devices also contributed to changes in working practices. Devices such as automatically reporting defect detectors, rear-end telemetry equipment for monitoring rear-end brake pressure and remotely setting brakes from the rear of the train, and a variety of improvements to the automatic air-brake system made a great impact. The mechanization of track maintenance afforded enormous changes in the methods of track building and repair. Individual worker productivity increased significantly, which resulted in the reorganization and trimming of maintenance forces.

Southern Pacific locomotive engineer Fred King strikes a pose as he takes a short break from kicking cars on the Bloomington, Illinois, yard lead, in the cab of SP GP35R No. 6639. While most newer locomotives come with air conditioning, many of the older four-axle units assigned to yard service are lean on amenities. *Steve Smedley*

Nickel Plate Road maintenance workers are pictured inside the company roundhouse at Conneaut, Ohio, in May 1957. Steam locomotives required a lot of men for daily maintenance and service. When the railroads became diesel-powered, they were able to close numerous small maintenance facilities and roundhouses. Jim Shaughnessy

The tender of a Burlington Route Mikado type is washed at the Galesburg roundhouse on November 24, 1956. Jim Shaughnessy

Baltimore & Ohio shopmen grease the reciprocating parts of a steam locomotive at Connellsville, Pennsylvania, on June 30, 1956. The high maintenance costs of steam locomotives contributed to railroads' eagerness to replace them with diesels. Jim Shaughnessy

A Burlington Route Class 0-5 4-8-4 locomotive receives a wash at the servicing facilities of the Galesburg, Illinois, roundhouse after a trip from Chicago on November 24, 1956. Jim Shaughnessy

DECLINE, REVIVAL, AND THE FUTURE

In the years following World War II, the railroads suffered great losses of traditional traffic. At that time, there was a renewed effort toward merger and consolidation of traditional companies as a means of combining and rationalizing facilities to save money and curb losses. Waves of mergers were implemented from the 1960s through the 1990s. A number of mergers took place between historic competitors such as the Erie Railroad and the Lackawanna, the Seaboard and the Atlantic Coast Line, and the Pennsylvania and the New York Central. Typically, railroad labor unions played a significant role in the negotiation of merger arrangements. Railroaders saw the writing on the wall: mergers spelled painful changes and the loss of traditional jobs and crafts, as well as the blending of seniority rosters. Doug Riddell wrote in his book *From the Cab*, "Mergers were never meant to benefit employees and frequently resulted in terms that pitted one worker against another, turned neighbor against neighbor, and in some cases alienated members of the same family." While deemed necessary to satisfy economic conditions, too often mergers imposed an immeasurable strain on individual railroaders.

Following mergers came route restructuring and the paring down of lines viewed as redundant, superfluous, or unnecessary. Whole routes were abandoned or downgraded. Yard and shops were consolidated and traditional facilities closed.

Along with consolidation came the trimming of branch lines and secondary routes that were deemed uneconomic to operate by traditional railroad agreements. Some were abandoned, while others were sold to new short line railroads. The working arrangements on short lines often differ from those on big railroads. Traditional craft lines were crossed and blended because just a handful of people were needed to perform a variety of different jobs. Some short lines began operations with little more than a single locomotive, a couple of customers, a handful of employees, and a few miles of track suffering from years of "deferred maintenance." To make a go of it, short lines needed to keep costs down and their heads high. Some new lines prospered and grew, while others floundered and were later abandoned.

From the 1970s through the 1990s, American railroads negotiated numerous changes with their labor unions. Crew sizes were reduced, operating districts extended, and craft distinctions were altered or eliminated. Sometimes change was negotiated by individual companies, or other times changes were implemented on a national level. Revision of traditional labor practices and increased worker productivity has been credited in part for the railroads' competitive revival in the 1980s and 1990s. Also significant was industry deregulation that began in the 1970s and culminated in 1980 with the passage of the Staggers Act.

During the 1980s, railroads enjoyed tremendous traffic growth. Heavy traffic is now largely focused on a handful of primary main lines where very long trains handle the bulk of railroad traffic. Yet, there are also hundreds of short line railroads serving smaller customers. Despite vast cuts in employment, numerous route and line closures, and the loss of many traditional types of traffic, North American railroads haul substantially more traffic today than they did during the traditional high-water mark generated by American involvement in World War II.

American railroad workers are now by far the most productive in the world. Traffic and productivity are at their highest levels, so railroads must carefully balance the need to keep trains moving 24 hours a day (and in all weather) with the needs of railroad maintenance and safe operating practices.

Traffic growth in the 1990s allowed the reopening of some lines that were previously closed. Large-scale investment by some railroads helped increase route capacity, which is dictated not just by the number of tracks, but by yard capacity, the ability to move trains efficiently with effective signaling and dispatching, and sufficient crew availability. A new generation of railroaders is now employed to move trains, and the numerous changes to the way they work have resulted in many changes in work rules and training practices. Today's railroaders incorporate a mix of experience that spans from the end of the steam era to the age of the mobile telephone.

New and emerging technologies, including advanced signaling systems, global positioning systems, and sophisti-

cated computer software are being investigated as means to enable further productivity gains. The pursuit of greater efficiency remains a measure of financial, if not social, progress. But does such progress always make things better for the individual railroader? In modern times, increased individual workload is often met with increased financial compensation, greater creature comforts, and fewer requirements for technical skill. Yet, in many cases, the old guard still feels nostalgia for days gone by, partly because the technology used to improve productivity reduces the skill levels needed to perform their jobs. Greater efficiency doesn't necessarily result in "progress" for everyone.

◐ On July 31, 1996—months away from his retirement—Southern Pacific yardmaster Kent Binkley concentrates on paperwork in the tower high above East Yard in Grand Junction, Colorado. In the background, a train carrying United Parcel Service shipments departs for Denver and points east. Tom Kline.

◑ Southern Pacific humpmaster Dick Rose works the retarder panel in the East Yard Tower on the afternoon of July 31, 1996, just a week before the Union Pacific merger that resulted in the closing of the Grand Junction, Colorado, hump. It was Rose's job to control the speed of freight cars coasting downhill off the hump during the building of freight trains in the yard. Tom Kline

In October 2005, Delaware-Lackawanna engineer Richard Janesko runs a former Canadian Pacific M-636 known as "Loretta." Beginning the day at Scranton, Pennsylvania, Richard and conductor Shawn Palermo take freight eastward on the former Lackawanna main line route. The route goes over the Pocono Summit to an interchange with Norfolk Southern near the Delaware Water Gap. Brian Solomon

A worker from Delaware-Lackawanna's Mechanical Department changes a light bulb in the number board housing on "Loretta" (M-636 No. 3643) at Scranton, Pennsylvania. A view inside the housing provides a good look at the class lamp lenses—white, green, and red—that were used on most Canadian locomotives. Brian Solomon

Buffalo & Pittsburgh machinists Doug Lowe and Todd Ritchie use an overhead crane to install a power assembly in GP18 No. 922 at Butler, Pennsylvania, in November 2004. Pat Yough

🎧 Jim Emerson at the 5-Hump in
Conway Yard in Pennsylvania uses
binoculars to spot car numbers in
August 2000. Mark Leppert

A Southern Pacific brakeman watches the meet
between his train and an eastward intermodal run from
the ground on SP's Sunset Route at Flatonia, Texas, on
January 24, 1993. Railroaders are trained to carefully

RAILROADING 101: BRAKEMEN

*B*rakemen were an integral part of both yard and road crews. *The craft got its name because a brakeman was literally tasked with applying and releasing train brakes. They were under the immediate authority of the conductor, and typically followed instructions given by the locomotive engineer. Because of its difficulties, dangers, and opportunities, the brakeman position is shrouded in lore, preserved in time, and glorified.*

One of the toughest and most dangerous positions on the railroad, it required an apprentice's level of skill, yet often was reasonably well paid. Working as brakeman offered a foot in the door to the world of railroad operations, while the transitory nature of the position made it an appealing profession for young men with wanderlust. After enduring and surviving his apprenticeship as a brakeman, a railroader could work his way up the ladder. In 1908, Calvin F. Swingle wrote in his book *Standard Rules for Movement of Trains*:

> As a rule, young men who decide to engauge in the rail-road service as brakemen do so because there is a certain fascination connected with the business, due to the fact that they are privileged to ride through various sections of the country, with advantages similar to those for which others have to pay, affording them an oppor-tunity to visit different villages and cities, which serve to satisfy the natural longing for travel and desire for change of scene felt by young men, especially between the ages of seventeen and twenty-five.

Lest the potential candidate for brakeman take Swingle's enticement to imply that the job was little more than an adventure disguised as a paid holiday, he continued with more advice:

> To make a good brakeman, a young man should be possessed of the average amount of good common sense, should have a good memory and a quick ear, should incline toward being shrewd and business-like, should be active, possessed of a sound body and a steady nerve. He should be firm in his decisions, following closely his instructions and looking to the best interests of the company, and should always be civil and polite.

Later, Swingle added:

> Instead of a young man, after entering the railroad service, "falling in" with the "rougher" class of men with the object of becoming "one of the boys," thinking that is the only way of securing friends among railroad men, drifting along until his will power is so weakened

A Rio Grande brakeman removes a marker lamp from the rear of a caboose on a narrow gauge freight at Alamosa, Colorado, on August 29, 1967. In accordance with the rules of the railroad, a train is not complete unless it displays markers. Taking off the markers signifies that the run is over. John Gruber

Working in the West Albany, New York, freight yards, a New York Central switching crew discusses their next switching move in April 1956. Each man carries a lantern—required equipment for brakemen. To make complicated moves, four- and five-man crews were required to pass hand signals to and from the locomotive engineer. Jim Shaughnessy

by dissipation that he has not the moral courage to leave his so-called "friends," and in preference, sacrificing his position, losing all ambition in life and becoming what is termed a "traveling railroad man," he should keep none but good company, and never miss an opportunity to gather information concerning the running of a freight train.

At the turn of the twentieth century, when American railroading was evolving into its classic form, an able-bodied young man could apply for the job of brakeman with hopes of beginning a railroad career. If he had no prior experience, recommendations from an experienced railroader could help convince a skeptical trainmaster or superintendent of his potential. He would find an official, fill out a rudimentary application, and take a basic physical exam. If the railroad accepted him, they would put his name on the brakemen's extra board and he would begin work with only rudimentary instruction, a wooden club, and an oil lantern. Over time, he would learn about the railroad and its procedures, rules, routes, customers, and history. The brakeman's job, like most starting positions on the railroad, provided its own training. A greenhorn brakeman would need to learn quickly simply to survive his employment, let alone to hope to collect his pay or advance.

TRAINING

Gone are the days of hiring brakemen off the street and sending them out on the road with little more than a flag, lantern, switch key, timetable, rulebook, and a pat on the back.

In those days, a brakeman position was treated as an apprenticeship to conductor, but it routinely took a period of years before a brakeman was eligible for promotion. Some brakemen might spend their whole careers on the railroad without anticipating or trying for the conductor's job. Today, most of the big railroads treat the conductor's position as entry-level railroading. Yet, due to the complexities of railroading, the strict nature of the rules, the prevailing culture of safety, and the enormous responsibility entrusted in a road conductor, new employees must undergo extensive training and testing before they can enter train service.

BEFORE AIR

Prior to the development and application of the Westinghouse automatic air brake, brakemen were needed to physically set train brakes upon signal from the engineer. On passenger trains, this was a relatively simple matter as a brakeman could travel from one end of the train to the other via the coaches' corridors to reach the brake wheels located on the platforms at the ends of the cars. Normally brakemen on passenger trains were dressed in a company uniform and expected to act in a courteous fashion toward passengers. When the train was in motion, a brakeman listened for two blasts of the whistle from the engine—the signal for "down brakes"—at which he'd jump into action, club in hand, and wrench the brakes down as quickly as he could. He had to make sure he didn't turn the brakes so tightly that the wheels locked up and slid. Sliding the wheels was not only damaging to the equipment, but it was ineffective for braking.

It was freight brakemen, in the formative era before automatic air brakes became standard equipment, who became the stuff of legends. In today's working environment, conditioned by safety and shaped by demands of comfort, it is virtually impossible to appreciate the job of the nineteenth-century freight brakeman. While his essential task was the same as a passenger brakeman's, the freight brakeman had to endure exceptionally harsh conditions. Freight cars have the benefit of neither corridors nor heat, and in order to perform his duties, a freight brakeman was required to ride the cars and be ready to set the brakes at a moment's notice.

Freight cars of the nineteenth century were typically wooden and equipped with catwalks on the roofs to allow brakemen to move from car to car. Brake wheels were positioned above roof level on long iron rods that attached to the simple brake rigging. This equipment, like the brakemen, was exposed to the elements and its condition could be expected to be rough at best.

When the engineer issued the two blasts for "down brakes," brakemen needed to jump into action and set brakes as quickly as possible using their clubs for leverage on the brake wheels. The only communication a brakeman could receive when the train was in motion was from the whistle—he had no way of knowing the circumstances for braking and needed to do his best to help the train stop. While brakemen were stationed at both the head end of the train and at the rear, they could not be in position to do their job if they were warming their hands by the firebox or lounging in the caboose. They were required to be up on the cars, regardless of conditions.

Too often, the brakeman's plight ended in death or maiming. One slip while running along a catwalk, or losing one's balance when the slack ran in, could send him tumbling. If especially unlucky, he would fall between the cars. Slipping was only one peril. Cold, wind, and rain might lead to hypothermia. Overhead hazards were another problem. Hopping from car to car against the direction of travel, he might not see an approaching overpass or tunnel as the train rolled along. To warn brakemen of overhead hazards, railroads erected "tell tails"—rods with rows of dangling string—before low clearances. When a brakeman felt the tickle of a tell tail, he had seconds to hit the deck. We can only imagine the spine-chilling sensation that a tell tail's strings would bring. Of course, most runs were made without incident, but over the years thousands of brakemen were injured and killed.

Peter Polus never took the conductor's exam and retired as a Chicago & North Western passenger brakeman when the Rochester 400 made its last trip in 1963. The young passenger climbing on the train in Madison, Wisconsin, is Paul Knutson of Lodi, Wisconsin. Polus, from Winona, Minnesota, hired out September 20, 1917. Passenger crew members typically wore military-like uniforms displaying the initials of their railroad on their lapels. John Gruber

On Northern Pacific's flagship passenger train, the North Coast Limited, running westbound as No. 25, the brakeman acknowledges "all clear" with a hand lantern at Little Falls, Minnesota, on April 19, 1959. William D. Middleton

The position of brakeman evolved as the Westinghouse automatic air brake became standard equipment, first on passenger cars, then gradually on freight as well. Considering the inconvenience and dangers of non–air brake trains, why were railroads so reluctant to implement air brakes? The simple answer is cost. Hundreds of thousands of freight cars were in service in the United States and it took years to either convert or replace non–air brake cars. For a number of years in the early 1900s, air-braked and non–air braked cars were operated together, and special considerations were taken in the makeup of mixed-brake trains. In 1900, The International Correspondence School's *Treatise on the Locomotive and Air Brake* explained:

> *In making up a part-air train, all the air cars, whether loaded or empty, should be placed together at the head end of the train and cut into service. Every air brake possible should be employed in braking, since the more in use the more smoothly the train can be handled; besides, they may be needed to make a quick stop in an emergency.*

Automatic air brakes greatly improved train handling and made it possible to safely operate much longer and heavier trains. Although air brakes reduced the number of brakemen needed to work those long trains, they did not completely eliminate the need for brakemen or immediately end the dangerous practice of walking on the tops of freight cars.

WORKING THE GROUND

Left: The rear-end crew climbs aboard caboose 086A during a Santa Fe crew change at Chillicothe, Illinois, in August 1984. Santa Fe was among the first big railroads to negotiate smaller crew sizes and longer crew districts. The change eliminated the Chillicothe crew change point. Crews now run through from Chicago to Fort Madison, Iowa, a distance of 228 miles. Steve Smedley **Right:** R. K. Chapman, conductor on CSX train J789, wades through knee-deep snow near Sidney, Ohio, after closing up main line switches on December 24, 2004. Railroaders, like postmen, have to work in all weather, including snow. Will Chapman be home for Christmas? Ryan Krengel

In yards and when picking up cars on the road, trains require brakemen on the ground to line switches and to couple and uncouple freight cars. A yard brakemen is normally called a "switchman," and a yard conductor may be referred to as a "yard foreman." On many lines there was a craft distinction between switchmen and road brakemen. Some railroads encouraged men to transfer back and forth between the yard and road rosters, depending on traffic demands.

In the yard, switchmen assemble trains. Making up trains involves the sorting and switching of freight cars, the latter of which requires brakemen to line up switches, uncouple cars, and set their brakes. Efficient switching also often requires

locomotives to "kick" cars, or help them roll independently onto various yard tracks. When groups of cars are assembled in the correct order, based on their common destination, they are known as "blocks." Traditionally when all the cars for a train were blocked, a caboose was attached at the rear and paperwork was readied for departure. In modern practice, a telemetry device that measures the brake pressure at the rear of the train and transmits this information to the locomotive has replaced the caboose.

Among the important railroad innovations of the late nineteenth century was the automatic coupler, first patented by Eli H. Janney in 1868 and commonly known as the "knuckle coupler." This device greatly improved the method of coupling and uncoupling trains. It also contributed to the operation of longer and heavier freight trains by improving the strength of the coupling between cars and reducing the amount of slack. In the link-and-pin days, brakemen coupled cars by dropping a pin in the holes between the links of the cars. To keep pace with the demands of railroading, this task was often done quickly, sometimes with moving cars, so a brakeman needed to be both nimble on his feet and deft with his hands. Brakemen were expected to be able to jump on and off cars traveling up to 15 mph. Failure could be costly; pins didn't always drop easily and removing them was tricky. The mass of a freight train moving at any speed is unforgiving to the human body—fingers were lost, bodies crushed, and lives ruined. An engineer could get his signals confused or a car could begin drifting unexpectedly, and a brakeman could find himself caught in between cars at the wrong moment. Across the United States, yards had tracks known informally as the "Slaughter" or the "Graveyard."

A New York Susquehanna & Western trainman climbs down from the cab of a GP18 on June 11, 2005, at Cortland, New York.
Brian Solomon

In the days before radio, men on the ground communicated with the engineer using a system of simple hand signals like those being given here by Frank Malcewicz on the North Shore at Rondout, Illinois, on June 15, 1962. The North Shore, a fast electric interurban line, also carried freight until it was abandoned in 1963. John Gruber

With the introduction of air brakes, the switchmen, under direction of their conductor or yard foreman, were also required to connect the air hoses between blocked cars and properly align their angle cocks (valves) to allow air to flow from one car to the next. Coupling cars and connecting air hoses each had their own hazards and challenges, especially in the days of link-and-pin couplers.

With the twentieth century came a much greater emphasis on safety. Rules were drafted, introduced, and modified to discourage hazardous practices, and men were admonished to follow the safe course. The role of the brakeman continued through the century as one of the primary operating crafts. Then as the decades progressed, changes in technology and work practices gradually made the position less essential.

While the engineer communicated with brakemen using whistle signals, the brakemen communicated instructions to the engineer using established hand signals. During the day, a brakeman would carry a flag and at night and in poor visibility, he would have a hand lantern. Standard hand signals as illustrated by Swingle in *Standard Rules for Movement of Trains* include:

Stop—moving the flag/lantern side to side at waist level
Proceed—vertically raising and lowering the flag/lantern
Back—swinging flag/lantern vertically in a circle across the tracks
Apply air brakes—swinging flag/lantern horizontally in a circle at arm's length
Release air brakes—flag/lantern held at arm's length above the head

Delaware-Lackawanna conductor Dave Heller prepares to unlock a switch as a former BC Rail Alco rolls by. Brian Solomon

Delaware-Lackawanna conductor Shawn Palermo compares his switch list with numbers on freight cars set out for interchange by Norfolk Southern. In addition to jotting down car numbers, he inspects each car, checks the condition of brake rigging, and looks for damage. Brian Solomon

In the pouring rain, Palermo sets a switch at Slateford Junction during a switching move to collect Norfolk Southern interchange. The switch has a large, yellow handle for ease of operation. Brian Solomon

AIR BRAKES

Today, the air-brake system is integral to most railroad operations. An air line known as the brake pipe runs the length of each car to charge reservoirs on the cars and they control the application and the release of the brakes. A reduction in air pressure applies the brakes. The system is designed for "fail-safe" operation, so if there is a sudden loss of air pressure in the brake pipe the brakes are automatically applied.

Normal operating pressure in the brake pipe is set at 90 psi for freight. While the brake pipe charges and actuates the brakes, the brake-pipe air is not used directly in setting the brake shoes on each individual freight car. This would take too long, causing the brakes at the front of the train to set up much more quickly than those at the rear. Instead, a valve on each car senses reductions in brake-pipe pressure and opens the reservoirs on the car that act on brake cylinders to put pressure on the shoes. In this way, the brakes set up relatively quickly and more uniformly throughout the train. (The system still results in a slight delay, with the brakes at the front setting up before those at the rear.)

The amount of braking action is proportional to the size of reduction in air pressure made by the engineer. Standard brake-handle positions allow for a minimum service reduction of 5 to 10 psi, a full-service application of about 20 psi, and a maximum emergency application. The latter evacuates the brake pipe as quickly as possible, reducing pressure to 0 psi and setting up the brakes much faster than normal. The emergency setting forces the brakes on and does not allow a rapid release; as a result, it is only intentionally applied when it is imperative to stop a train as quickly as possible and it is not intended for normal operations.

The name "emergency" has caused much confusion among non-railroaders over the years. An emergency brake application does not necessarily constitute an actual emergency or disaster. In addition, an emergency brake application can result unintentionally for a variety of reasons. A break in the air line, a faulty brake valve, or other mechanical difficulties can cause an emergency brake application.

A train is not ready to move until there is operating pressure throughout the brake pipe. Furthermore, a brake test must be performed and observed to ensure the system is operating correctly. The brakeman signals the engineer to apply (set) and release the brakes while observing brake-piston travel and the setting of the brakes.

Valves called "angle cocks" are located at the ends of cars where the air-brake hoses are attached to the air line. The handles are arranged so that when open, they are parallel to the hoses and when closed, they are perpendicular. This arrangement makes it easier to spot their position. When the angle cock is closed, it seals or "bottles" the air line and makes it impossible to set or release the brakes automatically beyond the point where it has been closed. It is necessary to close the angle cock at the end of a train or cut of cars to prevent the air from escaping. (Since the brake pipe is used both as an air delivery system for charging the reservoirs and for the control mechanism, it is crucial to keep the air from escaping.) By bottling the air, a car (or a cut of cars) can be positioned with the air brakes set and later joined with the rest of the train. After the air hoses are reconnected, a brakeman opens the angle cocks on each of the cars, which rejoins the air line. Since the air pressure had been retained in the various air hoses, less time is required to pump up the entire line to the correct operating pressure.

⟲ A brakeman rides the front of the hump set at Belt Railway of Chicago's Clearing Yard on July 1, 1995. Brian Solomon

🎧 Dave Heller connects air-brake hoses during a pickup at Scranton, Pennsylvania. The photograph also provides a good view of standard Janney knuckle couplers. Brian Solomon

In switching situations where cars are to be kicked, air brakes are disabled on those cars by releasing the brakes, isolating them from the train brake pipe with the angle cock, and completely bleeding off the air line. This process allows kicked cars to roll freely.

In the yard, a conductor (often known as a yard foreman) directs the engineer of a switching locomotive to kick a car that has its brakes released and isolated. Once the engine is moving, the brakeman uncouples the car or cars and rides them to where they need to be spotted. As they approach their desired spot, he winds down the handbrakes in traditional fashion. The handbrake is attached to the air-brake cylinder with a chain; by winding the brake down, tension on the chain forces the brake shoes to be applied. The handbrake is used for stopping rolling cars and for tying down stopped cars that have been spotted on a siding. It is not safe to leave cars unattended with only the air brakes applied and without the handbrakes set.

BRAKEMEN ON THE ROAD

In classic twentieth-century railroading, freight trains typically required two brakemen: a "head-end" brakeman and a "flagman" at the rear.

In the air-brake era, brakemen had several important duties; with the exception of the steam-era fireman, a head-end brakeman is historically the hardest-working member of any train crew. He worked the ground where he was responsible for lining switches, locking and unlocking derails, coupling and uncoupling during switching moves, and protecting the head end in the event of an abnormal situation or emergency.

On single-track lines where timetable and train-order rules were in effect, sidings were accessed with hand-throw switches. When required by his orders or schedule authority to "take the siding," the engineer would stop and the head-end brakeman would climb off, unlock the turnout with his switch key, manually line the points from the main track to the siding, and signal the engineer to proceed. As the locomotive chuffed past, the brakeman clambered back on, gripping the handrails and hoisting himself up. When the caboose was off the main line and was completely on the siding, the rear-end brakeman would restore the points for the main line. The brakemen on the ground gave the opposing train a "roll-by," to carefully look for defects such as dragging equipment, hot boxes, and shifted loads. If anything was amiss on the opposing train, they signaled the rear-end crew to stop.

On the move brakemen at both ends of a freight train were required to observe the train as they passed through curves. On the head end, the fireman and brakeman often divided this duty and watched for wisps of blue smoke from the wheel journals—a tell-tale sign of the dreaded hot box, which if left unchecked would result in a melted journal and a catastrophic derailment. Blue smoke wasn't always a hot box; more often than not it was just a sticking brake shoe. Either way, if they spotted a problem, the engineer brought the train to a safe stop and the brakeman went back to inspect the train.

If problems developed en route, it was the brakemen who climbed down from the locomotive cab or caboose to protect the train, or walked it to assess and solve problems. A

heavy freight might get a "kicker" and go into emergency. The slack would run in hard, sending men and merchandise crashing about. (One of the grave dangers of riding in a caboose was failing to brace yourself when the slack came in.) Operating men had the importance of protecting their train drilled into them. Failure to do so could quickly turn a minor problem into a catastrophe. In traditional "dark territory" on single-track, where there were no block signals protecting following movements, it was imperative that the rear brakeman—the flagman—protect the rear of the train. As Doug Riddell explained in a taped interview, "Flagman's primary responsibility was to protect the rear of the train. When the train stopped suddenly, you didn't ask any questions as to why you stopped, you grabbed your flagging kit, your fusees, your track torpedoes, and you hit the ground running. You were required to go back two miles to protect the train and you strapped torpedoes to the rail and lit the fusee to make sure trains had plenty of warning."

The brakeman would continue to protect until the locomotive engineer whistled for him to return. According to *Standard Rules for Movement of Trains* from 1908, the engineer gave one long blast and three short blasts when he needed a flagman to run back and protect the rear, and sounded either four or five short blasts (depending on the direction of the flagman from the head end) when he wanted the flagman to return. On a double-track line, even one protected by automatic block signals, it was imperative that a brakeman or other members of the crew protect the front of the train as well as the rear. An unexpected emergency brake application could be the result of a derailment. For all the head-end crew knew, their train might have spilled freight cars across the opposite track. A train racing the other way needed to be warned as quickly as possible to avoid colliding with the wreckage. Doug Riddell gave this account:

One night, when it was still double track—D-251 territory, movement in the current of traffic, you stayed to the right—from Richmond all the way to Rocky Mount on SCL, No. 3, the old Auto Train, the engine hit a truckload of cigarettes at the main crossing at Emporia and derailed. It was sliding sideways, the front end of the lead engine was over on the northbound track and it crossed the Meherrin River Bridge before it came to a stop. Andy LeGrand was the fireman, and the windshield broke and got glass in his eye. Aubrey

Delaware & Hudson conductor Jim Morrow and brakeman Walt Benjamine on caboose 35832 at the rear of a southward loaded ore train prepare to depart Tahawus, New York, on December 6, 1957. Jim Shaughnessy

Radio was one of the greatest labor-saving devices introduced to railroad operations. Delaware & Hudson brakeman Walt Benjamine uses his radio to advise the head-end crew 85 cars ahead to begin the journey from the iron and titanium mines at Tahawus to North Creek, New York, on December 6, 1957. Jim Shaughnessy

Walt Benjamine washes up on board caboose 35832. The caboose provided a place for the rear-end crew to ride, eat, work, and, after the run was completed at away terminals, to sleep. Jim Shaughnessy

Durrett was knocked unconscious. Raymond Weaver, the engineer, was almost seventy years old at the time, but he was a big husky man and knew his rules. He wasted no time and grabbed his fusees and his flag. He told Andy "you handle the radio" and he hit the ground running. Raymond ran a good three miles to flag down a north bound train.

Often the cause of an emergency application is relatively minor, but someone, usually the head-end brakeman, needed to walk the train looking for defects and attend to the problem as quickly as possible to get the train moving again. An emergency brake application is a violent event and the cars in the train reach a stop in a less-than-synchronized fashion. The cacophony of a freight in emergency is a deeply dreaded sound. The force of thousands of tons of metal slamming to a halt can damage even rugged freight cars. Inspecting a train requires a brakeman to look for damage to the couplers and drawbars. A weak point on all trains is the knuckle portion of the coupler, and a broken knuckle caused by slack running in may have caused the emergency application in the first place, or may have resulted because of the rapid stop. If it is not spotted and repaired, the cars will pull apart as soon the train begins

to move again. Spare knuckles and air hoses are usually stored on the locomotive or, in times past, on the caboose. It is easy to see why five- and six-man crews were common on most freight trains before the advent of radio, mobile phones, and other sophisticated audio communications. Large crews were also needed to set out and pick up cars where trains worked sidings and small yards, since it was necessary to relay (pass) switching signals around curves and in situations where it was difficult or impossible for the engineer to maintain eye contact with the man at the rear.

A Southern Railway brakeman stands by the switch into a lumber company at Hardleyville, South Carolina, on January 27, 1956, as the local freight's pair of Alco RS3 diesels pick up loaded cars. The brakeman on a local freight often spent more time on the ground lining switches and coupling cars than riding on the train. Jim Shaughnessy

BOOMERS

The nature of a brakeman's job gave him a transferable occupation, making him employable anywhere steel rails were laid. As with most railroad crafts, a brakeman's ability to hold work with a company was directly related to his seniority, which was traditionally established by the date of his physical exam. Most railroaders know by heart the day of their exam. The more employees that hire on after them, the more seniority they accrue, and thus their ability to retain work and choose assignments increases.

In boom times, railroads hired brakemen when traffic levels demanded more men to keep trains moving. Junior men worked from an "extra board" where their name came up in rotation. If his seniority permitted, a junior man would put his name on the board at the bottom of the list.

🎧 A CSX trainman lines switch train Y201 at Dayton, Ohio, on September 11, 1998. Note the portable radio on the man's hip. Bradley McClelland

When his name came to the top, he was assigned to a run. As an extra-board employee, he rarely knew who he'd be working with or on what train. The extra board had advantages for both the railroad and the brakeman. It gave the railroad a pool of employees that it could assign to trains as it chose. It didn't need to guarantee specific assignments, and that kind of flexibility is suited to the vagaries of typi-

cal freight operations because the tide of traffic and timing of trains fluctuates from day to day. The employee benefited from the extra board by being offered a variety of assignments. If he was new, it allowed him to learn different jobs and benefit from the experience of many employees. It also allowed him to earn a lot of money when business boomed. If he desired, he could work assignments back to back as long as the work held out, which the railroad often encouraged employees to do. Traditionally, operating men were not afforded weekends or paid holidays and they worked as often as the railroad provided assignments, within the federal hours of service provisions. As a railroader gained seniority, he was in a better position to bid for a regular assignment. This suited men as they grew older and became more settled, but it could take years of extra-board work before one held a regular position.

In many areas, seasonal traffic or fluctuations in the economy dictated when traffic peaked and when it tapered off. As the roster of assignments thinned, junior men were cut off but they could wait for traffic to resume or older men to retire. In the meantime they could take a holiday if their finances permitted, or find other work. Often young brakemen would follow the work and become "boomers." Transient by nature, boomers have long been characterized in railroad literature. The wanderings of Harry K. McClintock are recorded in the February 1955 issue of *Railroad Magazine*: "I left my seventieth milepost back along the road and have accumulated more nostalgia than money. I'm glad that in the years of my hot-blooded youth I was a boomer. I have seen a small part of this world and I wish I'd seen more." Harry worked as a brakeman for a host of lines, including Pennsylvania Railroad, Baltimore & Ohio, Northern Pacific, Southern Pacific, Union Pacific, and Santa Fe.

The life of a boomer was as varied as the migratory nature of the work would lead one to expect. Sometimes a boomer might find himself in the employ of a carrier for a number of years and develop a semi-settled lifestyle. More often than not, though, a boomer's life was spent in cheap trackside rooming houses, bunkhouses, and railroad hotels. He was on the road most of the time and he lived and breathed the railroad, for better and for worse.

Burlington Northern Santa Fe conductor Josh Smith tends to his paperwork on locomotive No. 715 in October 1998. Modern locomotives such as this General Electric Dash 9 have computers and desktop facilities. Locomotive crew comforts have come a long way since the days of open foot plates. R. T. Berryman

IN CHARGE OF THE TRAIN: THE CONDUCTOR

The senior position on any operating crew—regardless of age or seniority—is the conductor. The locomotive engineer pulls the throttle, but he doesn't make a move until the conductor indicates it is safe to go. The conductor is in charge of the train, its operation, and its safety. Traditionally, conductors were promoted from the ranks of brakemen. The two crafts represented a logical progression. The skills a young man learned as a brakeman would help him as conductor, a position that needed a thorough understanding of the mechanics and rules of operations. Brakemen experienced railroading from both the head end and rear of the train, as well as from the ground, in the yard, and on the road. A freight conductor normally rode in the caboose, which served as his office, lunchroom, and when at an away terminal, his bunkhouse. His primary concerns were operational logistics and accompanying paperwork. The duties of freight and passenger conductors varied but encompassed the same essential tasks of command, safety, and logistics.

Doug Riddell explains that a good freight conductor was the first one at the yard and reported for duty at least an hour prior to departure to ensure that his paperwork was in order. He inspected the train list that was issued by the yardmaster and which detailed the cars and their order in his train's consist. He reviewed waybills that showed what each car carried and its origin and destination, he inspected his timetable and train orders, and he worked out where the train would take sidings to meet, pass, or be overtaken by other trains, as well as where his train would work to make pickups and or set outs. If there was switching involved before departing or en route, he might make up switch lists for the brakemen describing which cars were set outs and where they were to be spotted.

A trainman is pictured on the back of a Rio Grande narrow gauge freight on August 29, 1967. The Rio Grande's narrow gauge lines in Colorado and New Mexico operated in a time warp and maintained traditional operating methods until the lines were abandoned. Today, a portion of this route is operated by the Çumbres & Toltec Scenic, a steam-powered tourist line. John Gruber

2 Nov 08

🎧 "Highball 31." The conductor gives Burlington Northern passenger train No. 31 the signal to depart North, La Crosse, Wisconsin, on April 20, 1971. John Gruber

Before departing, the freight conductor met with the engineer and brakemen to discuss their trip. He also walked—or "rolled"—by his train to inspect it for safety and compare the car numbers with those on the train list to make sure each was in proper order. Train make-up is crucial both for safety and the logistics of switching. As the train rolled by the home terminal, he boarded the caboose by swinging onto the rear platform. During the run he continued his paperwork and carefully checked any new orders received to work out how they would be implemented. Train orders simply and succinctly spelled out amendments to the

timetable in regard to operations. Often the mechanics of how the instructions were to be implemented were left up to the conductor. This responsibility did not mean he could do whatever he liked. Quite the contrary, the railroad's rules spelled out in detail how operations were to be carried out. It was up to the conductor to ensure the rules were followed in a safe and timely fashion. When a train ran afoul of the rules, the conductor was held responsible.

What may seem remarkable today was that, prior to the use of wireless communications, after a freight train departed its station or yard, the conductor had no direct means to communicate with the head end. He often did not speak to the engineer for the duration of the run. At the very least, the conductor could set the brakes in emergency—perhaps if the train was traveling too fast or had failed to stop at a designated meeting point.

TECHNOLOGY TRANSFORMS RAILROADING

While the transition from steam to diesel locomotives had a profound impact on operations, railroad shop forces, and the public imagination, it was one of only several major technological changes to profoundly affect railroads. Initially, dieselization had little effect on the nature of the conductor's job except for reducing the quantity of soot he needed to comb out of his hair at the end of a run.

The combined effect of other improvements, such as roller bearings, the welded rail, improvements to the air brake, Centralized Traffic Control, and clerical applications of the computer, have had an enormous impact on operations and have transformed the classic railroad into the modern one. Probably the most significant technological change for the conductor has been the use of radio and related technology such as rear-end telemetry and talking hot-box detectors. In the April 1958 issue of *Railroad Magazine*, Peter Josserand, a dispatcher for the Western Pacific, wrote prophetically, "The iron horse and Marconi's invention have become inseparable allies. At first, railroad communication was limited to men on the spot and the telegraph. Hand, whistle, and light signals offset this handicap. Then came the telephone, still later radio."

Today's freight conductor is a blend of several traditional crafts. In addition to the conductor's conventional responsibilities, he often serves as a brakeman and tends to duties once handled by the fireman, clerks, operators, and others. In the 1970s and 1980s, American railroads negotiated new labor and crew arrangements that reflected the changes made possible by technological advances. Road crews were reduced from five and six men to just two or three, and the distances they worked increased from the traditional 100-mile districts to, in many instances, 200 or 300 miles or more.

Use of the radio was gradually implemented in the four decades following the end of World War II. Initially used for communicating nonessential information among trains on the road, in the yards, and at stations, later the radio allowed men on the ground to speak with the engineer, which aided switching and superseded hand signals. Radio communication was eventually expanded to allow the dispatcher to communicate operating authority directly to the train crew without the need of intermediates, such as operators. A trainmaster for a large progressive western railroad explains, "The development of radio and the ability to use it properly greatly contributed to crew reductions. But this took time because initially crews were reluctant to use the radio."

Radio technology has numerous applications beyond basic person-to-person communication. Today, instead of a caboose, a telemetry device, commonly known as a "Fred" (flashing rear-end device) is used to transmit rear-end brake-pipe pressure to the head end and serve as a tail-end marker, with a flashing light to show that the train is complete. More advanced telemetry devices allow the engineer to set brakes from the rear of the train while in emergency or when a flaw in the brake pipe has bottled the air and prevented normal application of the brakes from the head end.

In addition, radio communication with other trains has eliminated the necessity in many railroad rules for crews to physically protect the train when it has stopped unexpectedly. Centralized Traffic Control, radio dispatching systems, and modern rules are intended to ensure that trains do not follow each other so closely that there is a risk they may collide. Coincident with these technologies, safer operations have stemmed from the universal applications of roller bearings that have greatly reduced the instances of hot boxes. In addition, automatic reporting detectors that measure journal temperatures are useful for the detection of dragging equipment and high and wide loads. Such appliances have essentially replaced employees on the ground and in the cab who visually inspected trains for defects. Computers have eliminated thousands of clerks who once processed the mountains of paperwork that accompanied the movement of freight.

The transition from classic to modern railroading and the evolution of the modern conductor's job has taken decades, and it is still changing. Today, personnel from the old school work alongside a younger generation that knows only the modern methods.

A conductor in a Union Pacific caboose shouts, "Don't snap my picture! Okay, you got me!" The scene took place east of North Platte, Nebraska, in June 1976 as several westbound trains were backed up and waited to get into the huge Bailey Yards. Steve Smedley

CSX Conductor John Gunter logs onto the company computer to begin his workday at the Lynchburg, Virginia, Sandy Hook Yard office, a former Chesapeake & Ohio facility. Gunter will work the local based out of Lynchburg switching industries along the James River Subdivision. Doug Koontz

John Gunter started work for CSX predecessor Chesapeake & Ohio in 1951. On a locomotive at Lynchburg, Virginia, with radio in hand, his duties today include a variety of tasks once handled by firemen, brakemen, and conductors. Crew reduction, made possible by technology such as radios, has transformed the industry. Doug Koontz

A conductor completes paperwork on a Norfolk Southern freight caboose near Lynchburg, Virginia. Doug Koontz

Maryland Midland's Dan McMaster performs a brake test at Highfield, Maryland. The telemetry device on the back coupler shows brake-pipe air pressure at the rear of the train. Doug Koontz

Dan McMaster gives radio instructions to the engineer and rides the pilot steps of a locomotive as it switches cars at Highfield, Maryland. Doug Koontz

ONE CONDUCTOR'S VIEW

Greg Cruickshank hired on as brakeman with Penn Central at the railroad's sprawling Selkirk Yard south of Albany, New York, on July 15, 1974. This was a dark time on the railroad. Penn Central was a leviathan created in 1968 by the merger of New York Central and Pennsylvania Railroads, and it was saddled with the financially destitute New Haven in 1969. The combination was fraught with problems from the onset and it resulted in the largest bankruptcy to date in 1970. Its track, locomotives, and traffic suffered from neglect. Yet in this environment, Cruickshank learned railroading.

He explains that from Selkirk Yard near Albany, New York, you could work several different directions on former New York Central lines. East took you out on the old Boston & Albany over the Berkshires; west sent you along the Mohawk Division of Central's Water Level Route toward Syracuse and Buffalo. There were two routes south, with one on each shore of the Hudson; the busier of the two routes was the old New York, West Shore & Buffalo, known in modern times as the River Line. Cruickshank says, "My first trip was down the River Line. They just told me to report for duty. I knew nothing. I didn't even know where the River Line went, but at that time on PC it was possible for a brakeman to work without a clue as to what was going on. There was no schooling, education, or test. You learned the job by the good graces of the people you worked with."

The Penn Central bankruptcy and the deteriorating financial situation of many lines in the East had forced

Congress to take action in an effort to prevent further weakening of the industry. On April 1, 1976, Penn Central joined other bankrupt eastern lines in the federally sponsored bailout known as the Consolidated Rail Corporation, or Conrail. Billions of government dollars were spent to upgrade lines, buy new equipment, and get the railroad back on track. This revitalization took years to accomplish, and in its early years Conrail wasn't noticeably better off than its predecessors. After the transition to Conrail—in which blue paint gradually replaced PC's grimy black—and four years' experience as a brakeman, Cruickshank took a promotion to conductor following a test in autumn 1978. As a brakeman, and later conductor, he routinely worked the B&A, a heavily graded line that is the antithesis of New York Central's typically water-level lines. Railroading here presented its fair share of challenges as eastward freight trains weighing as much 7,500 tons struggled over the line with decrepit diesels suffering from poor maintenance. Cruickshank recalls his work on the B&A fondly:

Working the B&A had its advantages despite lower pay than either the River Line or the Mohawk. The B&A crews were good people. When you got to Boston, the engineer would ask you to join him for dinner. You were kept active and really did some work as many trains set out at Pittsfield, West Springfield, Worcester, Framingham. Generally the B&A involved daylight runs, while the River Line and Mohawk were largely night work. We worked seven days a week.

In 1974, when I started, radios were still rare, but after Conrail they become standard. On PC, the head end had a radio, but not individuals. Sometimes the conductor rode at the back in the caboose, and other times he rode the head end. Later it was required for the conductor to ride the head end.

⊙ On February 10, 1961, an Erie-Lackawanna commuter train conductor waits on the platform for a tardy passenger at Hoboken Terminal, New Jersey. The train cannot depart until the conductor gives the signal to go. Jim Shaughnessy

⊙ Metro-North conductor E. J. Duffy at Peekskill, New York, on October 2, 1999. Patrick Yough

In the PC era the equipment was falling apart. The locomotives were in bad shape. Coming up the grade we had all kinds of problems. Bells would be ringing in the cab warning you of ground-relay problems, low water, and low oil. Often we had old GEs. They were nice and warm, but didn't do very well. We had a lot of trouble with the tonnage going east. Working as a brakeman or conductor you needed to go back and make minor repairs en route. When a ground relay tripped, you would go back [to the unit with the problem] and reset the switch. We needed to do whatever it took to keep the locomotives running. This type of thing had typically been the fireman's job.

Once a lucrative cash cow, one of the big money losers for Conrail and its predecessors was the suburban passenger business. Although this business was subsidized in part by the states since the 1970s, Conrail wanted to be rid of this side of railroading, and in 1983 it got out. Conrail operations on its former New York Central and New Haven lines to Grand Central Terminal were conveyed to Metro-North Commuter Railroad, now MTA Metro-North Railroad. Despite nine years in freight service, Cruickshank made the move over to Metro-North as a passenger conductor. After working both freight and passenger trains, he has some interesting observations:

When I started as a passenger conductor, the job required just two days of revenue classes. Today, a new hire in passenger service gets five weeks' training, and it requires six to seven weeks of classes for a promotion to passenger conductor. The jobs are entirely different. In freight service you look at the railroad, you watch the tracks in front of you or behind. As a passenger conductor you only see out the side windows and you very rarely see the railroad. Instead, you're dealing with the people. You meet some really nice people on the job, but

some really awful ones, too. As with all conductors, a passenger conductor's first priority is for the safe and efficient movement of the train. You are responsible for the safety of both its crew and its passengers. You need to keep the train running on time. In addition to that, you also need to collect and sometimes sell tickets.

A passenger conductor gets paid better than a conductor in freight service, and with passenger work you never get dirty, plus you can sleep in your own bed every night. But there's a trade-off—passenger work is high-stress. But you rarely have to do things like get out on the ground and cut out a sticking

brake—which we used to do all the time in freight service on PC when the equipment was bad. Yet, when I look back, I had a great feeling of accomplishment working freight on the B&A.

Suburban passenger services were not the only operations Conrail spun off in the early 1980s. Like other big carriers of the period, Conrail looked to pare down its system to focus on the heaviest lines. It sold many branch lines and secondary routes to short line companies. One of these, the Pioneer Valley Railroad in the Pinsley short line railroad family, began operations in 1982 on a couple of former New Haven Railroad/Holyoke & Westfield branches that connected with Conrail at Westfield, Massachusetts. Today, although it operates less trackage than it did at startup, Pioneer Valley remains a thriving short line serving 12 to 15 regular customers in the Westfield area using secondhand CF7 diesels from the Santa Fe Railway. Since the 1999 breakup of Conrail, its primary interchange is now with CSX.

Pioneer Valley employs a host of enthusiastic, dedicated employees who operate their trains and maintain locomotives and track. Among them is conductor Larry Runyon, who comes from a railroading family. His grandfather was a brakeman on Baltimore & Ohio, his father was a section foreman for Baltimore & Ohio/Chesapeake & Ohio, and his uncles also worked for the railroad. Before going to Pioneer Valley a few years ago, Larry worked for Central Vermont for ten years and Massachusetts Central for five. A freight conductor on a short line is a very different job than either a passenger conductor on Metro-North or a freight conductor on a big railroad. Larry explains, "On a big line, you report, hook, and pull—away you go. On a short line, like Pioneer Valley, you make up your own train. We are customer friendly here. I like that, but you have to think quick. If a customer changes their mind about which cars they want delivered, you have to know where your cars are and make a spot change in the setup of your train."

Larry does the jobs traditionally performed by a conductor, brakeman, and customer service representative. He handles paperwork, works out where cars are going, and sets up his train, all while working the ground—setting switches, lining up couplers, connecting air hoses, pulling pins, and tying down handbrakes. It's demanding work, and performed in all weather, but Larry thrives on it:

◖ Burlington Northern Santa Fe's Sheldon Kaneko rides aboard locomotive LMX 8538 on August 9, 1998. R. T. Berryman

◗ Pioneer Valley Railroad conductor Larry Runyon compares a switch list with his train list and transfers data from one to the other. Brian Solomon

I like switching. I have a lot of energy and I don't want to be sitting around. I'd rather be on the ground thinking. Winter is good; snow doesn't bother me, rain doesn't bother me. We're worse than the postman! Early starts are okay, too. The earlier, the better. There's less traffic on the roads and on the crossings. It's peaceful, and with an early start we'll get off work earlier. We're usually on duty 10 hours, but they try to get us out in eight.

I decide who gets which cars. [I] start with a switch list in the morning, [then] we make up our train and go. With a short line, you meet your customer, you know the guys unloading the cars, you work with them, and it makes the day so much nicer.

Pioneer Valley is largely a switching railroad. It originates and terminates cars that are then passed off to CSX. They handle a little bit of intra-line traffic as well. The radio is integral to Larry's job. With it, he communicates instructions to his engineer as he works the ground. The engineer is largely a technician in this capacity. He executes instructions given to him by his conductor, but he doesn't necessarily worry about the next series of moves as they put together their train in the yard.

CONDUCTORS ON THE ROAD, YESTERDAY AND TODAY

Traditionally, a way freight stopped at every little town along its route and spotted cars at local industries, warehouses, small-town freight houses, and team tracks. These trains carried both carload and less-than-carload (LCL) business. A 30- or 40-foot slide-door boxcar would deliver LCL freight of all descriptions to freight houses where it was stored until the customer came and collected it. A freight agent handled the paperwork and dealt with customers. Team tracks were used to spot cars for loading where customers didn't have their own tracks. Grain hoppers or refrigerator cars in twos or threes might be loaded with produce from local farmers. In his book *High Green and the Bark Peelers* (about the Boston & Maine in the late 1940s), author R. M. Neal describes a day out with the Hillsboro (New Hampshire) local freight that ran from the yards at Lowell, Massachusetts, to its namesake town. Hauled by a single 2-6-0 Mogul-type steam locomotive, this typical small-town way freight was in its twilight years and gives a splendid view of how things were done in days gone by. The nostalgia leaves Neal with mixed feelings on the viability of local railroading that once provided the vital link between small-town America and the markets of the nation and the world. Neal wrote:

We pass a few farms, and come in sight of an occasional surfaced highway, twisting and narrow, thereby an adequate testimony that this region simply doesn't need a railroad any more, hasn't the population

to support one . . . . At South Milford we cut out a tank car at the Standard Oil plant. Buckley (the fireman) tells me we must drop more cars soon, because "the big hill" is so steep that seven or eight cars are the most the Mogul can drag. Suppose we had a dozen cars? "We'd pull six or seven to the top, leave them, and come back for the others," he answers.

At Milford we get rid of some L.C.L . . . . Conductor Tilton and Brakemen Sargent and Savage are busy with hand trucks, trundling these little shipments out of the local or way car. Buckley isn't required to help, but the day is hot and he knows the train crew will be perspiring, so he, too, helps with the unloading. I look at the boxes and crates and other goods in the local car.

A wheelbarrow is going to Hillsboro. Some gallon cans of Sears Roebuck paint are in transit to Antrim. We have two boxes of General Electric light bulbs, other boxes of Kleenex. A carton of crepe-paper Halloween cups from the C. A. Reed Company of Williamsport, Pennsylvania, is part of our freight. Plumber's equipment for John J. Carey is in one corner of the car. Near a door are cans of poultry feed. A box of Hallmark greeting cards is in the car. We are carrying garden hose, too. Spiegel's mail-order house at Chicago has given us a shipment of small furniture, crated. A Montgomery Ward canoe is another of our items.

A box car on another track has Milford's new and glistening fire truck. It came yesterday and hasn't been unloaded yet.

Neal concluded that there is some life yet in the old Hillsboro Branch, "The communities, few and mostly

Continued on page 68

Upper: Conductor C. L. Manro busies himself with his newspaper during a quiet moment on the westbound journey of Fargo–Streeter, North Dakota, local train No. 139 on April 20, 1959.
Lower: Frank White, the conductor on the Jamestown–Oakes, North Dakota, mixed train No. 154 completes his paperwork between stops on April 20, 1959. Mixed trains were local freights that also carried passengers. Once common across the nation on lightly traveled branch lines, mixed trains largely disappeared with the advance of highway transport. Photos by William D. Middleton

Northern Pacific motor car No. B-21, operating as Fargo–Streeter train No. 139, makes its stop at Verona, North Dakota, on April 20, 1959, to handle mail and express traffic. William D. Middleton

Mark French works the ground in front of a graffiti-covered Golden West boxcar during a switching move near Corning, California. California Northern crews begin their run by collecting freight cars and assembling their train. Brian Solomon

On the morning of July 7, 2005, conductor Mark French discusses his switch list with engineer Tim Holbrook at Corning, California. California Northern is a short line that operates a disconnected group of former Southern Pacific secondary main lines. Brian Solomon

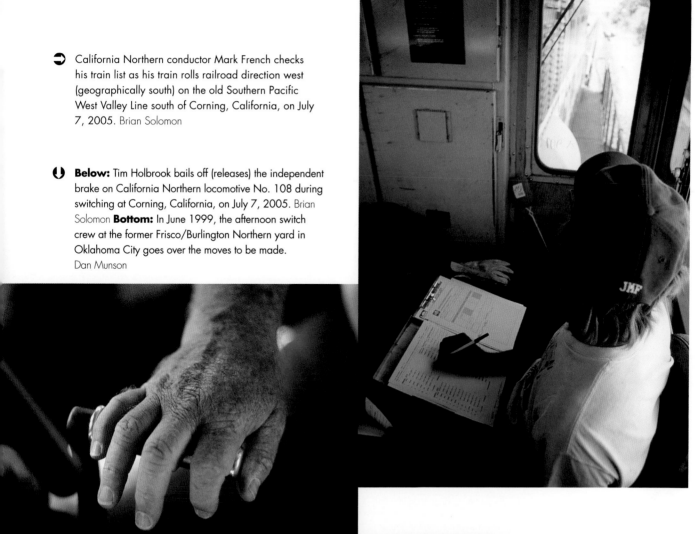

○ California Northern conductor Mark French checks his train list as his train rolls railroad direction west (geographically south) on the old Southern Pacific West Valley Line south of Corning, California, on July 7, 2005. Brian Solomon

○ **Below:** Tim Holbrook bails off (releases) the independent brake on California Northern locomotive No. 108 during switching at Corning, California, on July 7, 2005. Brian Solomon **Bottom:** In June 1999, the afternoon switch crew at the former Frisco/Burlington Northern yard in Oklahoma City goes over the moves to be made. Dan Munson

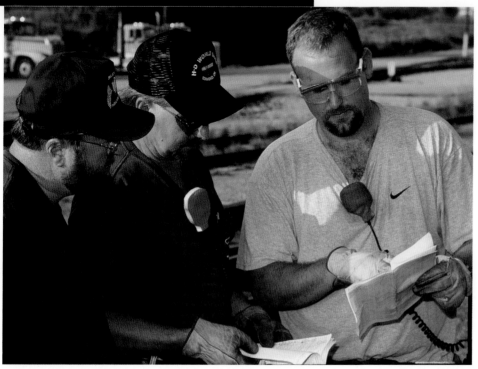

Continued from page 64

small, that cluster beside [the Hillsboro Branch] need our local train."

In his book *From the Cab*, Doug Riddell tells of working as brakeman on Seaboard Coast Line's Ahoskie local in the rural North Carolina Piedmont in the late 1970s:

> [B]eing a workhorse way freight, the Ahoskie Local (No 2. 493-494 in the timetable) delivered cuts of local traffic to Weldon and Boykins, picking up anything there destined for points in eastern North Carolina. Between Boykins and Ahoskie, there seemed to be an endless array of manufacturing plants, farm cooperatives, and wood yards at the ends of rusting, weed-hidden spur tracks, reaching out like long slender fingers from the slightly better maintained rails of the Lewiston and Ahoskie subdivisions. This was railroading as it used to be, before the big boys opted to throw the baby out with the bath water—abandoning localities it once vowed to serve to concentrate on mainline unit train and intermodal long hauls. I guess it probably meant nothing to the clerks in the billing department at Jacksonville, Florida, but if they could have seen the look of satisfaction on the face of the crusty old farmer at Severn, North Carolina, on my first trip, when we spotted a flatcar laden with a huge, green and yellow John Deere combine in the house track, they would surely have shared his excitement.

The very nature of railroading has evolved. The railroad's customers have changed, and so the local freight has changed, too. In the past, a local delivered small shipments to small customers; now it delivers large cuts of cars or even whole trains to big, often national customers, and forwarding agencies. Instead of the customer being a small-town hardware store, it might be a national chain. Even if this customer just receives one or two carloads at one location, this might represent just a fraction of that customer's business on a national level.

Today, progressive larger railroads encourage their local crews to work with their customers. Often the conductor is the interface between customer and railroad. But instead of speaking with a man on a loading dock, he may communicate with a service rep at a centralized location—often hundreds, perhaps thousands, of miles from the point of delivery. The conductor finds out where the car or cars need to be spotted and if there is anything else the railroad can do to help the customer. If a car is delayed en route, the conductor advises the customer of the delay and when the car should be expected.

Typically on the big lines, a switch crew in the yard makes up the train using a computer-generated switch list put together by a yardmaster. This list is a detailed account of which cars need to go out on a specific train, the order in which they should be assembled, and the yard tracks on which they are located. Each car carries the initials of its owner and a unique identification number. Traditionally, railroads owned most of the cars, and each railroad had a letter abbreviation by which it was known, such as "PRR" for the Pennsylvania Railroad, "NYC" for New York Central, "CNW" for Chicago & North Western, and so on. Today, many cars are owned by non-railroads. Sometimes these are large customers such as electric utilities or grain cooperatives, in other cases they are leasing firms. Non-railroad cars usually have an "X" at the end of the abbreviation. The switch list indicates the car IDs and types, which cars are empty and which are laden, and some type of destination. Since railroads often interchange cars, the destination on the switch list may be a car's interchange point rather than a final destination.

On the road, a conductor carries a train list. This list is a computer-generated manifest that lists the cars in his train. Like the switch list, this identifies each car by its initials and ID number, and includes the car weight, length, and type, whether it is laden or empty, contents, its destination or block information, and also if it contains any hazardous materials, and, if so, what kind of load. Hazardous materials cars, known as "haz-mats," have a variety of special considerations depending on the type of materials carried. If the train is expected to pick up and set out cars, the conductor is also issued a set out and pickup list as part of the train list.

➲ Delaware-Lackawanna conductor Shawn Palermo rides the back of a lumber car being delivered to a reload facility at Cresco, Pennsylvania. Brian Solomon

Over the course of his journey, the conductor marks up his train list to reflect switching moves, pickups, and set outs. Since the weight and length of a train directly affects operations, it is crucial that the conductor calculates the make-up of his train as changes are made and reports them by radio or company telephone to the dispatcher. When ascending and descending long grades, the weight of the train determines the amount of power needed to move it and the level of braking needed to keep its speed in check. The length of the train determines which sidings the train will fit into, which can also affect how the dispatcher handles it over the road.

While local freights spend the better part of their day switching out customers and working small yards along the line, road freights often make pickups and set outs as well. It is common practice on many of the large railroads for road freights to pick up at interchange points with other lines and make block swaps en route with other road freights. Such pickups and set outs may consist of one car or cuts of 100 cars or more. In addition to attending to switch and train lists, a modern freight conductor often acts as the interface with the dispatcher when copying crucial paper work such as track authorization. The engineer *may copy*

track authority given over the radio, but he *may not* do so when the train is in motion.

Another responsibility of the modern conductor, inherited from the duty of fireman and head-end brakeman, is calling signals. When the engineer spots a line-side signal he is required to call out its aspect, which is echoed by the conductor as a confirmation of the aspect even if the conductor is not in a position to see the signal himself. Some railroads now require the engineer to call out over the train radio the aspect, name or number, and track of each signal as it is observed, in order to warn other trains in the area of its presence. On BNSF, conductors must fill out a signal awareness form that lists each and every signal by milepost location that the crew operates over. Every signal must be marked, and the conductor must indicate the speed of the train when passing any signal displaying an aspect more restrictive than "clear."

While many road freights now operate with just two-man crews, some still carry a third person, usually to assist with switching in situations where a single man on the ground would be ineffective, inefficient, or dangerous.

Continued on page 73

Delaware-Lackawanna conductor Shawn Palermo looks out into the rain from the front of No. 3643 as the PT98 approaches Tobyhanna, Pennsylvania, to pick up empty liquefied petroleum gas (LPG) cars and a laden timber car. Brian Solomon

One of Shawn Palermo's duties as conductor is to connect air-brake hoses and open angle cocks to fill the brake pipe on cars like these being switched at Tobyhanna, Pennsylvania, on October 13, 2005. Brian Solomon

Despite its widespread demise, the caboose survived on some runs into modern times. R. T. Berryman and J. Nelson ride the caboose on Burlington Northern Santa Fe's inside gateway route, the Gateway Subdivision, at Westwood, California, on November 1, 1999.
R. T. Berryman

A C&NW conductor rides the caboose on a Jefferson Junction local. This train still carried a caboose into the 1990s because it needed to make long reverse moves. Employees are not supposed to ride the ends of freight cars, so cabooses were provided for safety. Brian Solomon

Continued from page 69

RADIO CONTROL OPERATIONS (RCO)

In the last few years, some of the bigger railroads have introduced radio control operations (RCO) technology that has effectively blended the positions of conductor and engineer and allows for one-person switch crews. It is impractical for the ground work to be done remotely, so instead RCO technology has placed the engine controls on a portable console handled by the man on the ground. As with other new technologies, the introduction of RCO has been controversial. Some railroaders have viewed it suspiciously and see it as potentially dangerous and inefficient.

A trainmaster at a progressive western railroad argues otherwise and puts the technology in perspective: "The introduction of RCO will have [a comparable] effect on operations as did the introduction of radio 30 years ago. It's good technology *if* you know how to use it. If [crews] don't know how to use RCO, then it's of no use. But when they do, it's a real benefit."

With RCO, the conductor controls the movement of the locomotive. He has portable throttle and brake controls. Instead of speaking over a radio, instructing the engineer to pull ahead or telling him "three cars to the hitch," he makes the locomotive move himself. Initially, some users found the technology frustrating because the console and locomotive didn't always respond as hoped. Yet, learning efficient operation with the new technology is possible.

Burlington Northern Santa Fe switch foreman Steve Volts operates SD40-2 No. 6915 using radio control operations (RCO) technology at Argentine Yard, Kansas City, Kansas, on February 4, 2003. Photos Dan Munson

At sunset on May 20, 1995, a Wisconsin Central
train crew finishes their run at Valley, near Fond du
Lac, Wisconsin. Under the direction of Ed Burkhardt,
Wisconsin Central purchased a sizable fleet of
second-generation Electro-Motive Division diesels,
including former Santa Fe No. 5959. Brian Solomon

CHAPTER

3

AT THE THROTTLE: ENGINEERS AND FIREMEN

*T*he best known and most admired of all railroaders is the locomotive engineer. The envy of boys everywhere since the first locomotives gasped steam and chuffed forward, the engineer, with his hand on the throttle, controls the locomotive's power. In the nineteenth century that was a 4-4-0 American-type steam locomotive; today, it is a state-of-the-art high-horsepower diesel-electric.

In a classic scene, the Canadian Pacific engineer on Royal Hudson No. 2857 looks westward at Guelph Junction, Ontario, on August 3, 1957. In the left pocket of his coveralls are the company rulebook and timetable. His glasses, gloves, and hat were standard apparel to keep out the cinders that rained down. Jim Shaughnessy

With his left hand on the throttle and his right on the whistle cord, Tutland Railroad engineer Ray Haseltine runs Alco RS-1 No. 401 on the Rutland, Vermont–to–Catham, New York, local freight. Jim Shaughnessy

In the early days, locomotive crews were afforded little more than a platform at the back of the engine. Today, modern locomotives are equipped with climate control, ergonomically friendly working environments, and comfortable seats. The crew on the foot plate of South Eastern & Chatham Railway No. 65 operates on Britain's preserved Bluebell Railway. Brian Solomon

The engineer also gets the locomotive over the road and brings it to a safe stop again. Manipulation of the brakes is where a good engineer really comes into his own. Keeping a 14,000-ton coal train under control while winding down a mountain grade or bringing a passenger train with hundreds of people on board from 110 mph to a precise station stop takes a lot of training, skill, and nerve. As Metro-North engineer George W. Kowanski explained in an interview, "Running a locomotive is not like driving a car—it's like nothing else."

As with all aspects of railroading, evolving technologies have changed the way engineers run locomotives—this was true 100 years ago and it will be true 100 years from now. In the formative era, the locomotive engineer was afforded little more than a platform at the back of the boiler on which to stand. His controls were primitive and simple. He had a throttle to control the flow of steam from the boiler to the cylinders, a "Johnson bar" or similar mechanism used to "hook up" or regulate the valves (which was how he controlled the speed and direction of the locomotive), and a simple engine brake to stop the train. Over

At 6:20 p.m. on February 23, 1957, the engineer of Canadian National locomotive No. 5293, working train No. 23 from Sherbrooke to Montreal, is poised with an oil can to lubricate the machine's reciprocating parts. Steam locomotives required constant attention from their crews. Jim Shaughnessy

time, additional devices became standard, including a whistle and bell both to warn people of the train's approach and to communicate with its crew. As locomotives advanced, automatic water pumps, feedwater heaters, sanding devices, and lubrication equipment were added to make operation more efficient.

Throughout their 125-year reign, steam locomotives became larger, faster, more complex, and vastly powerful. Yet, the basic principles of running a steam locomotive remained the same. An engineer working an old, saturated-steam 2-6-0 Mogul hauling a short train of wooden cars on strap-iron rail had the same basic skills that were needed to

get a massive 2-6-6-6 Allegheny or a fast 4-6-4 Hudson under way decades later on steel rails. Stopping these trains, however, was another story altogether. Toward the end of the 1800s, the development and application of the automatic air brake was one of the greatest changes in train handling in the history of the railroad.

STARTING STEAM

With a clear road ahead and a signal from the conductor to go, the steam engineer sets the valves for forward motion, releases the brakes, and cracks the throttle. With a hiss and the bark of the smokestack, the locomotive comes to life and inches forward. Starting out, the dynamics of adhesion must be considered carefully. Steel wheel on steel rail relies on adhesion by friction for successful application of rotary motion. Without adhesion, the drivers slip. When starting a steam locomotive with its enormous driving wheels, the engineer gradually increases power just the right amount. If the locomotive begins to slip, the engineer notches back the throttle to regain control.

Starting out on level track with dry rail is tricky; starting out on a grade or in the rain requires patience, skill, and sand. Spreading sand on the rail improves adhesion and reduces the chances of wheel slip. In the early days, a brakeman or fireman laid sand down manually by carrying a bucket and spreading sand in front of the locomotive.

As technology advanced, sanding became more efficient and sophisticated. Late-era steam locomotives typically feature one or more sand domes above the boiler with lines running down to direct the flow of sand to points immediately ahead of the driving wheels. In autumn, crushed leaves on the rails are a curse. Leaves get pounded into a greasy paste that often causes locomotives to lose traction.

➜ On August 7, 1958, Norfolk & Western's Blue Ridge pushers wait at Boaz siding, east of Roanoke at the west end of the Blue Ridge grade. Pushers were cut on here to shove loaded coal trains over the hill. There are two pusher crews.
Jim Shaughnessy

Steam locomotives use double-acting cylinders, meaning that steam acts on each piston face in turn as it moves back and forth inside the cylinder. As steam pushes the piston in one direction, exhausted steam exits in the other. As the locomotive gains speed, it reaches a point where exhausted steam cannot exit the cylinder fast enough, resulting in back pressure that retards the piston's forward motion. To overcome this, the cutoff point is reduced so that steam only enters the cylinder during a portion of the piston's power stroke. A skillful engineer controls locomotive speed by adjusting the cutoff rate and makes only minor adjustments with the throttle. At high speed, the valves may be set to just 25 or 30 percent cutoff. Years of experience were required to master this skill.

Continued on page 84

On the evening of August 7, 1958, a Norfolk & Western fireman with a lantern at Boaz siding east of Roanoke near Vinton waits with Y6 Mallet No. 2129. N&W was an anomaly in mid-twentieth-century American railroading. It resisted dieselization longer than any other main line carrier in the United States, and it designed and constructed its own locomotives until the mid-1950s. It was finally dieselized in 1960, a full decade later than some other railroads. Jim Shaughnessy

The crew of a double-headed Norfolk & Western coal train exchanges greetings with the crew of a Mallet pusher waiting at the Boaz siding on August 7, 1958. Jim Shaughnessy

A Norfolk & Western Blue Ridge pusher calls at Boaz siding. N&W was the last railroad to build and operate Mallet compounds in main line service. Jim Shaughnessy

For the helper engineer on the foot plate of a N&W Mallet at Boaz siding lunch consists of a Thermos of coffee and a plastic bag of cheese and crackers brought from home. Jim Shaughnessy

Boaz siding was a pusher base at the west end of the railroad's Blue Ridge grade. Norfolk & Western's Y6a Mallet No. 2160 waits to push a coal train on August 7, 1958. Jim Shaughnessy

A road foreman exits the telephone shack at the N&W helper siding at Boaz siding, while the crew of a big Mallet waits for the next eastward coal train to shove over the Blue Ridge. Note the extra knuckle at the base of the shack. Jim Shaughnessy

Continued from page 79

STEAM FIREMEN

Traditionally every locomotive had two enginemen: an engineer and a fireman. The fireman was vital, and his title described only those duties relating to his work tending the fire in the boiler. In the early days of steam, this meant physically shoveling coal from the tender. Later, advanced locomotives had more sophisticated means of delivering fuels. Coal-fired steam locomotives (a number of railroads, especially in the West, had favored oil-fired steam locomotives) had devices such as automatic stokers that used a powered screw to carry coal from the tender and steam jets to deliver coal into the firebox.

The fireman also monitored the boiler pressure, kept the boiler full of water, and made sure that safety devices such as water sight glasses were clean and functioned properly. In addition, he was responsible for blowing down the boiler to remove the buildup of impurities and for cleaning ash pans below the firebox.

Every steam locomotive was a time bomb waiting to explode if it was not tended properly. If the water level in the boiler got too low and the top of the firebox known as the crown sheet was exposed, the result would be catastrophic. A boiler explosion was among the most feared accidents of the steam era. As with so many aspects of railroading, a fireman needed to maintain balance between safety and efficiency. Too much water in the boiler and it wouldn't function properly; too little water could cause it to blow up. At the firebox, the fireman needed to know where to place coal to its best effect. Dumping too much in the wrong place would prevent it from burning properly and wasted coal. It would also cause dense black smoke and would not produce sufficient steam when the engine was working hard.

The fireman was also responsible for the locomotive's running maintenance, keeping the cab clean, sweeping the foot plate of stray coal, and wiping down the controls and interior surfaces. When the locomotive stopped at stations or sidings, the fireman filled the tender with water from wayside tanks and water plugs, lubricated reciprocating parts, and kept the drive rods and other equipment clean. More advanced locomotives had appliances like hydrostatic lubrication systems that aided firemen in their duties. In the cab, while shoveling coal and working the injectors or water pumps to keep the boiler full, the fireman was also expected to "call signals," a safety practice whereby he echoed the engineer to ensure that both men knew which aspect had been displayed on the wayside signals they passed.

Like the brakeman, the fireman was a typical entry-level position on the railroad. Reference letters in hand, a young man with a strong back and a desire to enter train service would seek out a trainmaster, road foreman, or roundhouse foreman and find a place on a fireman's extra board to begin his education. Some railroads required little or no training for greenhorn firemen, assuming that engineers would oversee their actions. Other lines such as the Pennsylvania Railroad were more rigorous and required firemen to have road knowledge and be qualified before they were allowed to work on their own.

Although often unstated in the fireman's contract, an important part of his position was his role as an apprentice engineer. His trade of fueling and maintaining the engine were preparatory skills for running it; his work with the engineer offered the opportunity to learn running skills and to become familiar with the peculiarities of the railroad. It was assumed that ambitious young men would learn from the older men by working with them. They would develop not just the ability to make the locomotive move, but all the techniques and nuances of train handling. During a relative lull in his duties, the fireman might be asked to try his hand on the right-hand side of the machine.

This apprenticeship system was not expected to train new engineers overnight. Quite the contrary, it routinely took years. A man might shovel coal for a decade or more before he could expect to be qualified as an engineer and accept promotion. In fact, in steam days, a fireman might remain just that—either he would be content in his position or aware that there was little opportunity or likelihood of promotion. Career firemen were commonplace.

Continued on page 88

The fireman on Canadian Pacific Royal Hudson No. 2857 looks forward as they work west of Guelph Junction on August 3, 1957, with Pacific-type No. 2236 helping. Jim Shaughnessy

The fireman on Nickel Plate Road Berkshire No. 774 waits for the signal to depart Conneaut, Ohio. Jim Shaughnessy

Lettin' off Steam

By Doug Riddell

In the beginning, there was the steam locomotive. For over 100 years, it symmbolized the American railroad. Post-World War II dieselization not only changed the face of the industry, it abruptly and forever altered the lives of engineers and firemen who began their careers shoveling coal, but ultimately climbed down from cabs of sleek first-generation diesel-electric locomotives to collect their pensions.

As returning servicemen and their families abandoned coach seats for private automobiles, and truckers siphoned off short-haul and less-than-carload freight business using federally funded Interstate highways, railroads pressed their unions for more pay and work rule concessions. With postwar workforce levels ample to handle wartime traffic, a full generation passed before it became necessary to hire new employees. Today, few remain who worked in both steam and diesel. Those who do, often express mixed emotions because the transition was concurrent with sweeping changes throughout the industry. In more ways than one, it was truly the end of an era.

"The only people who reminisce about the 'romance' of the steam locomotive are those who never had to fire one," stated engineer Rob Yancey, who was best friend and frequent fireman for fellow Seaboard Air Line locomotive engineer John Cutchin. In the late 1970s, I was privileged to fire for them on Amtrak's *Silver Meteor*. Though both have now passed away, they regularly mesmerized me with intriguing tales of life aboard the SAL's Q Class Mikes, which typically powered their 16-hour,

7-days-a-week workhorse road switchers on the road's Virginia Division in the twilight of steam.

"Railroading's no different than life. We remember the good times and try to forget the bad. There's nothing like the sound of that whistle moaning in the night," Cutchin smiled, lighting his pipe as he kept a watchful eye on the diesel's speedometer. "A steam locomotive cab could be the hottest place under the sun during the summer, and the coldest place on earth in the winter."

"As a fireman, there was an art in knowing how to keep the fire red-hot and the steam pressure up. It was a matter of pride," Yancey commented. "And as a reward, when everything was just right, and you had a moment to lean on the armrest to check the exhaust from the stack, you sensed the raw power your locomotive was producing. You could see the drivers, the rods, and the pistons. Unlike the diesel, there was nothing to hide or muffle the sights, sounds, and smells of your engine working."

Yancey went on to make clear that whether he was using steel wool to polish the backhead or employing a shovel to free up the jammed paddles of a cantankerous Elvin stoker, there was always something to be done and it was back-breaking work. "The railroads thought that when diesels came along, there would be no need for a fireman," he said. "But there were still steam generators to keep lit on passenger trains, and even on freight trains, a diesel fireman spent a lot of his time making running repairs. And engineers are not just born and don't just walk in off the street. They have to be trained, and there's no substitute for experience at the side of an experienced locomotive engineer."

In addition to requiring individually crafted replacement parts, steam locomotives had to be stopped frequently for coal and water. Diesel parts came off the shelf and the internal combustion growlers were limited only by the amount of fuel their tanks could hold. Small towns, like Rob Yancey's home of Norlina, North Carolina, became mere listings in a timetable with no more steam engines to service. Using diesel engines meant relocation to points further down the line.

Would Yancey have preferred to give up diesels and return to steam? "Mrs. Yancey didn't raise no dummies," he grinned. "I could fire a steam locomotive with the best of them, and I loved to run them when I had the chance, but there's something to be said for coming to the end of your run on a diesel, not covered with coal dust, no holes burned in your clothes from

cinders, and no blisters on your hands from handling a shovel. And I hear diesels today are even air-conditioned."

On the evening of February 23, 1957, the fireman on Canadian National J-7-b Pacific-type No. 5293 waits to depart Sherbrooke, Quebec. The steam pressure is up and safety valves have lifted. The canvas behind the cab helps keep out blowing snow. *Jim Shaughnessy*

Continued from page 85

DIESEL-ELECTRICS BRING CHANGE

The greatest change to American railroad operations in the twentieth century came about with the transition from steam to diesel power. This development fundamentally altered the way railroads operated trains and resulted in many changes to the maintenance and manning of locomotives. Diesels were more efficient, more reliable, and more flexible, and required far less heavy maintenance compared to steam.

Diesels utilize a complex combination of petroleum and electric technologies. Successful operation of a diesel-electric engine requires manipulation of the diesel prime mover and electric systems in an efficient manner. The goal is to take the best advantages of both without incurring damage to the equipment. The throttle regulates both the speed of the diesel's engine and the output of the electric generator that provides current to power the electric motors. American diesel-electrics use a stepped (or notched) throttle on which each of

the running positions matches the engine and generator output characteristics to provide efficient operation and avoid overloading either system. An ammeter shows the level of current going to the traction motors so the engineer can avoid overloading them for a prolonged period. (In the course of ordinary operations, it is often necessary to overload motors for short periods to get a train moving or to keep it moving in heavily graded territory. The length of time a motor may be overloaded is known as its "short-time rating.")

As technology matured, diesel manufacturers and railroads gradually improved these machines while developing methods of training engineers to run them more efficiently.

The diesel engines—the prime movers—were more powerful, a great deal more reliable, and much more efficient. The electrical systems were likewise improved. New technology was developed to simplify diesel-electric operation and reduce the possibility of accidental damage to motors and prime movers as a result of normal operation.

Each steam locomotive had required its own crew, which greatly increased the expense of adding more than one locomotive to a train. One of the great advantages of the diesel-electric is the ability to connect locomotives together using multiple-unit technology. Operating diesels in multiple allows railroads to make major adjustments in the amount of power a single engineer can wield without the need to increase crew size. (Technically, the diesel locomotive is considered the combination of individual diesel-electric units. In modern operation, most units are equipped with an operator's cab and can function singly as locomotives. However, in the early days

railroads ordered diesel-electrics with and without cabs; those with cabs were designated "A" units and those without were "B" units. In some situations, as with Electro-Motive Division's pioneering freight diesel, the model FT, the A and B units were semi-permanently coupled with drawbar connections. In part, this was done to address concerns by the railroads that labor would insist on having men assigned to each and every unit.) Also, since the diesel's operating characteristics allow it to start a much heavier train than was possible with steam, diesels led to the operation of longer and heavier trains while greatly reducing the need for manned helpers to get the trains started.

The advent of diesels required engineers to learn new skills and adjust the way they ran trains. Ultimately, diesels reduced the number of people required to operate locomotives, which fundamentally and forever changed working practices and traditional training methods.

Upper: On October 2, 1964, the engineer on the Rio Grande's Train No. 10, the Yampa Valley Mail, blows the horn of the big PA diesel. **Lower:** Diesels were a radical change for head-end crews. While some men were nostalgic for the old steam locomotives, diesels offered a much cleaner, quieter, and more civilized work environment. Sitting in the cab of an Alco PA diesel, the engineer on Rio Grande's Yampa Valley Mail reaches for his watch to check the time of departure. Photos by John Gruber

A New Haven Railroad engineer boards a nearly new FL9—its nose and builder plate gleaming—on a southward passenger train at the station in Hartford, Connecticut, in July 1957. The FL9 was a unique model because it was designed and built for the specialized requirements of the New Haven. Jim Shaughnessy

Chief road foreman of engines Martin Davis rides high in a nearly new Delaware & Hudson Alco C-628 No. 602, the first of the series to be delivered to D&H at Colonie, New York, in April 1964. Jim Shaughnessy

DIESEL FIREMEN

The motive power transition posed many changes for enginemen. The working environment was a dramatic change. Certainly some men had nostalgia for steam, but others liked the perks of the new diesels. Henry Kitchen, a fireman who hired on with the Seaboard Air Line in 1941 and worked between Raleigh and Richmond and Raleigh and Portsmouth offered this perspective on the transition: "Diesels were much cleaner, for one thing, and more comfortable, too. Steam was very, very hot in the summer and very cold in the winter—believe it or not. Even with that boiler there, it was cold because the locomotive was very open."

The relative ease of operating a diesel locomotive compared to steam made the role of fireman seem redundant to many who had never worked in engine service. Railroads were keen to take advantage of the potential savings made possible by eliminating redundant personnel. However, early efforts to eliminate the fireman's position were stifled by the necessities of train operations and the need to negotiate with the firemen's union. Despite apparent redundancy, the fireman's position was initially retained.

Early diesels kept the fireman pretty busy. Alco's FAs and the earliest Electro-Motive F units had manually operated radiator shutters that required periodic adjustment to keep the engine temperature within safe operating limits. Also, early diesels were relatively cantankerous machines that needed constant attention. Low-water alarms, ground relays, and engine over-speed mechanisms routinely tripped. When bells rang in the cab, the fireman was dispatched to sort out the problem, which could be as simple as resetting a circuit breaker or bridging out a traction motor using switches on an interior electrical panel. Yet, often it required

that more complicated, messy work be performed as the train slugged along. Usually the trained fireman was also sufficiently proficient in operations and could take over in the unlikely event that the engineer became ill or was otherwise incapable of running the train. In fact, one of the most valuable roles of the diesel fireman was his position as trainee engineer. As the engineer's apprentice, the fireman typically spent thousands of hours in locomotive cabs before being

⊃ **Upper:** On August 25, 1995, Wisconsin & Southern (WSOR) engineer Paul Swanson keys the radio on his GP9 as he heads west of Waukesha toward Janesville, Wisconsin, on the old Milwaukee Road. Railroads are always looking to improve employee safety; today, high-visibility clothing is required of WSOR train crews. **Lower:** Engineer Paul Swanson gets off his Wisconsin & Southern GP9 at the end of the day on August 25, 1995. Short of its terminal at Janesville, the crew of this freight ran out of time as prescribed under the Federal Hours of Service Act. Today, train crews are limited to a maximum of 12 hours on duty. Photos by Brian Solomon expected to assume the role of engineer. During this time, he gained a comprehensive and thorough understanding of locomotive operation and the complexities of train handling. He also became intimately familiar with the territory that he was expected to run. Before being promoted to engineer, Doug Riddell worked as a brakeman, fireman, and hostler. "There is *no* substitute for experience," he states. His opinion is brought home by a phrase often uttered by most locomotive engineers: "Every train is different."

George W. Kowanski, who hired on with Penn Central on January 5, 1971, and worked former New York Central and New Haven lines around New York City and Southern New England, describes his experience as a fireman:

I stumbled into the job as a locomotive fireman. I just wanted to work for the railroad—it was my lifelong ambition. You were an apprentice engineer—there were no engineer's training programs at that time. You learned by doing whatever the engineer told you to do.

Some engineers were not very sociable, but the good guys were mentors to you. At the time I hired out, some of these guys were nearly 70 years old—they were like a grandfather to you. One was Jimmy Berwaldt, a fascinating guy, a gentleman, and a really nice old man. Growing up in the Pelham Bay area of The Bronx he remembered when [the New Haven] put the wire up on the Harlem River Branch around 1912 and when they six-tracked it. He was in the Navy during World War I and hired out with New York Central about 1926, where he fired the old Shays [geared steam locomotives] on the West Side Line. He told me lots of stories about working through the streets with the "Westside Cowboys." These were brakemen who rode horses with red flags and preceded every freight train down 10th and 11th Avenues. The freights were limited to 10 miles per hour and limited to about 25 cars, so there was a constant parade of trains.

The first week I was on the railroad, the engineers put me in the seat to give them a break. We were in the yard and the switching could be pretty monotonous. We'd be switching for four, five, six hours without a break.

In the early 1970s, the railroad still didn't have everyone radio-equipped and we still used hand signals. [In New York City] when we used to leave the West Side Freight Line with a road job—the road jobs were made up between 110th Street and 79th Street on the east side of the tunnel on what they called the "Wall Track"—we would leave 72nd Street with our power and go up to 110th Street. There, we would wait for a signal to back onto our train, then couple up, tie on, and pump up the air. But we did the brake test with hand signals. There would be car inspectors strung out in the tunnel. Since the tunnel had gradual curves in it, you needed three or four men between the head end and the caboose, and these guys passed signals on the fireman's side. The signals from the head end [were] "Apply," horizontal motion with the lamp, [and] "Release," lamp held high. When the test was completed they would give the engineer, "Okay on the brakes"—a twirl of the lamp. That's how we did our brake test. Now the whole place is just a memory.

Traditionally, the progression from fireman to engineer wasn't always straight-forward. Even when a fireman was qualified to work as an engineer, it didn't guarantee engineer work right away. A fireman only got "set up" as an engineer when the railroad wanted him. Furthermore, some firemen were reluctant to accept promotion because firemen and engineers had different unions and worked from different rosters. A fireman promoted to engineer would find himself at the bottom of the engineer's roster, and thus get the least desirable jobs. Kowanski was a fireman during the transitional period when PC began to phase out the position and introduce new methods of training. He was among the first Penn Central employees to attend engineer's training. Kowanski first worked as an engineer on July 4, 1976, after Penn Central had given way to Conrail.

Improved locomotive design and new technologies, combined with the desperate and worsening financial condition of many American railroads in the early 1970s, contributed to a reevaluation of the freight fireman's position. In 1972, American railroads negotiated an arrangement with operating unions to lower craft barriers and allow the promotion of brakemen and conductors into engine service. This did not immediately retire the freight firemen, but it was a step toward eliminating the position. Initially, most railroads continued to employ firemen, and some even continued to hire them until the early 1980s.

Continued on page 96

Metro-North's George W. Kowanski runs locomotive 230 (GE Genesis dual mode) with train No. 8840 on September 24, 2005. With almost 35 years of service, Kowanski has witnessed a transformation of the industry and its work practices. Patrick Yough

George W. Kowanski in a classic pose on FL9 No. 2016 at North White Plains, New York. Patrick Yough

Engineer Jim Berwaldt works the throttle of an Alco switcher at 72nd Street Yard in Manhattan. His seniority date was July 31, 1925. George W. Kowanski

In New Haven, Connecticut, engineer Henry Frackiewicz takes the throttle of a GG1, the power for train No. 169. Like many railroaders, Frackiewicz was from a railroad family. His father was a machinist on the New Haven at Oak Point motor storage at 149th Street in The Bronx. Frackiewicz hired on July 1, 1941, but served in an army transport unit during World War II in North Africa, Sicily, and southern France. He was a mentor to George W. Kowanski and taught him the nuance of locomotive operation. George W. Kowanski

🎧 The head-end crew gets off Santa Fe SD40-2
No. 5705 at the end of the run at Chillicothe,
Illinois. Steve Smedley

Continued from page 92

PASSENGER FIREMEN

Through the 1970s and into the early 1980s, firemen were still employed on long-distance passenger trains, which were then owned, marketed, and financed by Amtrak, but at the time still operated with host railroad crews. Among their duties, passenger firemen tended steam-heating equipment used to provide train heat and hot water. Steam generators on diesels were a carryover from the steam era, when the locomotive boiler was used for heating. By the 1970s, decades of heavy use and less-than-ideal maintenance had taken their toll on the old diesels that Amtrak inherited for passenger duties. Doug Riddell, who worked as a fireman on Amtrak, explains, "With those old E8s, you'd stay back there the whole trip. You wouldn't even see the cab of the locomotive. They were falling apart. You were either working to keep the prime movers going, or working with the steam generator."

The steam generators used diesel fuel and firemen needed to know their intricacies, including the wiring and plumbing diagrams. George Kowanski recalls the difficulties of working with steam heat:

I was coming out of Boston on Thanksgiving Day 1974 or 1975. It was bitterly cold, maybe 10 to 15 degrees, and we had about 14 to 16 cars—a real mish-mash—P70s and everything else. [On the head end] we had three ex-Pennsy E8s, each one of which had two steam generators. These weren't maintained all that well and I had a helluva time keeping the steam up on the train. Back then, the rule of thumb was you wanted 10 pounds [pressure] on the gauge for every car in the consist, so with 14 cars, you needed 140 pounds on the steam gauge. When we left Boston we had just two steam generators running and these gave up right away. So I had to run back through the units to get two generators running, and stay running to build up pressure so the train wouldn't freeze up.

One problem was that there would be a pressure drop as the steam made its way back through the train. You might have 140 pounds coming out of the engine,

but very little pressure at the rear. The danger with this was that you could have a steam line freeze up at the rear. Once the lines froze, they were difficult to thaw out. I was going back and forth between the three E units all the way to Providence. Once you got to know the steam generators, you could usually tweak them to get them to work.

The adoption of head-end electrical power (HEP) eliminated the need for steam generators. First used by commuter railroads, in the 1970s HEP became the new standard for Amtrak equipment. By 1982, all the steam-heated equipment had been retired from regular service. A few railroads such as Metro-North and Canada's VIA Rail continued to employ steam heat for a few more years. Operating people shed few tears at the loss of steam heat, but with HEP there was much less work for the passenger fireman.

Many late-era firemen were hired for the express purpose of being trained for engine service. In 1985, the fireman's position was officially negotiated away at the national level. Remaining firemen were to be eliminated by attrition and promotion. The need for railroads to improve productivity and cut operating costs to improve their competitive position justified the loss of the position. New training programs filled gaps once handled by the old apprenticeship system.

But there are other considerations perhaps overlooked at the expense of improved productivity. As Doug Riddell explains, "The loss of the fireman is unfortunate from a safety standpoint. On the freight railroads they have an engineer and a conductor up on the engine, but on Amtrak we [now] have just one man in the cab. The conductor is back riding the train. You need a second person on the head end who knows how to run."

He continues, "Late at night [or] early in the morning when it's cold and there's snow and you have the heater running, it's hard to stay awake and concentrate, and there's so much going on. At times like that, I miss having a second man in the cab."

IN THE SEAT

"Anyone can run a train—the tough part is starting and stopping it," Riddell says with a serious look in his eye.

Today, engineers are typically promoted from the ranks of conductor. Engineer training is rigorous, thorough, and includes three intensive months in the classroom, work with simulators, on-the-job training in the locomotive, and strict testing. In the old days, it might have taken a fireman 10 to 20 years of working in the cab under the tutelage of experienced engineers before he was promoted to engineer. Today's newly promoted conductor may very well become a qualified engineer, too, assuming he or she passes all the exams in little more than a year's time.

The result is that modern engineers are professionally trained and federally licensed, but often have less real-time experience in the seat than did their predecessors when they make their first solo run. More than just the training has changed—modern technology has been implemented on virtually every level of railroad operation. Computers monitor, regulate, and "optimize" every aspect of locomotive operation. Microprocessors maximize fuel efficiency, limit harmful emissions, protect mechanical and electrical equipment—including traction motors—and thus prevent operation that equipment designers have deemed either potentially damaging or dangerous. But computers don't always work perfectly. More than one train has been stranded because of a minor computer fault.

Automation has taken a degree of control away from the individual. A computer merely follows its program and is not receptive to persuasion. In many situations, technological changes have also reduced the skill level once required to operate trains. Kowanski, who now works with dual-mode (diesel-electric/electric) Genesis diesels and electric multiple-units in New York suburban service, elaborates:

> I've worked on GG1s and E8s and none of [these new machines] are even close by comparison. With a GG1, you were an extension of the machine. There was a level of nuance and you needed to concentrate on what you were doing. When you ran these machines you could feel what they did in the seat of your pants. It was an incredible experience. The guys really prided themselves on train handling. With the newer trains, you do not have the freedom of control that you once had. A lot of things are done by the computer for you and it's more difficult to run the train smoothly. You no longer need to have the level of skill that you used [to] have. Now the computer does it for you. [Back then] you had to learn more to [run] well. The job has been dumbed down and it's not the same anymore. It's much easier.

Yet, braking still requires a skilled engineer and remains one of the most difficult parts of the job. For the past 100 years, the air brake has been the standard mechanism for stopping a train. Typically, locomotives are equipped with two sets of controls: one is for the train brake, the other for the locomotive brake, known as the "independent" because it uses a separate brake pipe operated independently of the train air.

Before an engineer can move a train on the road, he or she must be assured that the brakes are working properly. This check is achieved through the brake test. The rules for brake tests have changed over the years and vary depending on the type of train and the crew conditions. In essence, a brake test is necessary whenever there has been a substantive change to a train's consist or crew. In addition, on very long freight runs brake tests are performed at intervals as part of an overall inspection of the equipment. (Freight trains were traditionally inspected every 500 miles, but today some runs only require inspections every 1,000 miles due to improvements to braking equipment and car design.)

Air brakes are normally in the released position with the brake pipe maintained at maximum operating pressure (currently 75 psi for yard, 90 psi for freight, and 110 psi for passenger) when the train is rolling. To set the brakes, the engineer makes a reduction in brake-pipe pressure using his train-brake handle on the control stand. Older brake schedules (6, 24, and 26 brake handle/valve arrangements) were designed to exhaust a jet of air directly into the cab as a confirmation that the system was working properly and to give the engineer a feel for braking.

The engineer at the throttle of New York Central's former Cleveland Union Terminal electric No. 235 leads the famed *Empire State Express* northward (railroad direction west) out of Grand Central Terminal toward Harmon, New York, on April 13, 1957. Jim Shaughnessy

Yet, this exhaust can be deafening. Modern brake schedules reduce brake pressure electronically and replicate the hiss of air release. With modern air-brake equipment, a normal brake application—known as a service reduction—typically takes 10 to 20 pounds of pressure out of the brake pipe. Valves on each car are designed to sense a change in brake-pipe pressure. With the reduction in pressure, the valves respond mechanically by releasing a corresponding amount of air from storage reservoirs on the cars to the brake cylinders, which apply pressure to pistons that act on the brake shoes to grip the wheels and slow the train. It takes a moment or two from the time of the reduction until the slowing of the train can be felt in the cab. To release the brakes, the engineer moves the brake handle to the release position, which restores air pressure to the brake pipe that draws from a reservoir on the engine. Valves on the cars then respond by moving the brake cylinders to remove pressure from the shoes. Releasing brakes also involves a delayed reaction.

It may take several minutes for a full release. Due to the delay in response, the engineer must be very familiar with his brake and the line over which he is running, as well as be able to anticipate the need to slow down or stop. Riddell explains, "In regards to train handling on the road, you have to think so many miles ahead."

🎧 Despite adoption of advanced communications, in some situations earlier methods such as hand signals are still used. Burlington Northern engineer Wayne Logan leans out the window to observe his brakeman's hand signals while switching as he talks with the yardmaster over the train radio at Casey, Texas, on February 28, 1988. A veteran railroader, Logan started his career on the Erie-Lackawanna in the 1960s by running trains out of Gary, Indiana. Changing jobs brought him to Texas, where he has spent many years working on the North Houston switcher. Tom Kline

Keeping the train stretched during braking is important for smooth operation. If the slack runs too quickly as a result of braking, it can cause damage to the train or its freight, or injure passengers. When the train brake is applied, the independent brake is automatically applied as well. Often, the engineer neither requires nor desires the extra braking force of the independent brake. To avoid the ill effects of having the train bunch up behind the locomotive, he releases the independent shortly after applying the train-brake air—an action known as "bailing off the independent." This action causes the cars behind the locomotive to brake, but not the locomotive.

Many books have been written about the use of the air brake, but the nuance of braking technique is something that must be learned through experience. Riddell says, "I don't operate a train like anyone else and I don't know any two people who operate the same way. Everyone has their own style." He adds, "Putting the train brake on is like a rubber band. I feel and visualize the slack in between the cars' brakes setting down on the rear of the train, and as they begin to set up and pull on the train. It's like a chute at the drag strip—there's a force slowing you down. You're pulling against the train and there's a force slowing you down that keeps it stretched out so there's no slack."

While basics of the braking systems are essentially the same, passenger work has different considerations than freight. Riddell describes some of his considerations:

When working a passenger train you have specific stopping points [at stations]. You develop specific points to set up the brakes, so when you're coming into a station, as you pass a certain stanchion on the platform you know to make a full-service reduction. Yet because no two trains are the same, even if you have the same engine and the same cars on the same run that you had yesterday, temperature and humidity affect your braking. So during the first few minutes of running you find if you have a good-braking train or a poor-braking train. To run effectively you need to know your train.

Technological changes to locomotives have included significant advances in air-brake technologies and the development and advancement of dynamic braking systems. The introduction of the pressure-maintaining valve is another good example. In the old days of automatic air brakes, once an engineer made an initial service application (reduction in brake-pipe pressure), ordinary leakage in the brake pipe caused the brakes to gradually apply more and more, and ultimately stop the train unless the air pressure was restored to release them. It was much more difficult to regulate train speed, especially when descending a prolonged grade. With the pressure-maintaining valve, an engineer can make a service reduction of 10 to 20 psi and expect it to remain at that level without the need to release the brake. It becomes much easier to control the train and reduces the risk of using up the air too quickly as a result of repeated application and release.

Continued on page 104

◐ **Upper left:** Operating a locomotive is a learned skill. In September 2005, Pioneer Valley engineer Al Massey has his left hand on the throttle of a former Santa Fe CF7 while working the yard at Westfield, Massachusetts. **Upper right:** Engineer Al Massey shuts down CF7 No. 2558, the City of Westfield, after a full shift switching industries around Westfield, Massachusetts. The CF7 is a model converted from an Electro-Motive streamlined F unit and it is well adapted to yard work. **Lower left:** The view from the cab of Pioneer Valley Railroad CF7 No. 2558 includes locals passing in the yard at Westfield, Massachusetts, in September 2005. Train crews on Pioneer Valley work together to switch freight cars and serve their customer. Photos by Brian Solomon

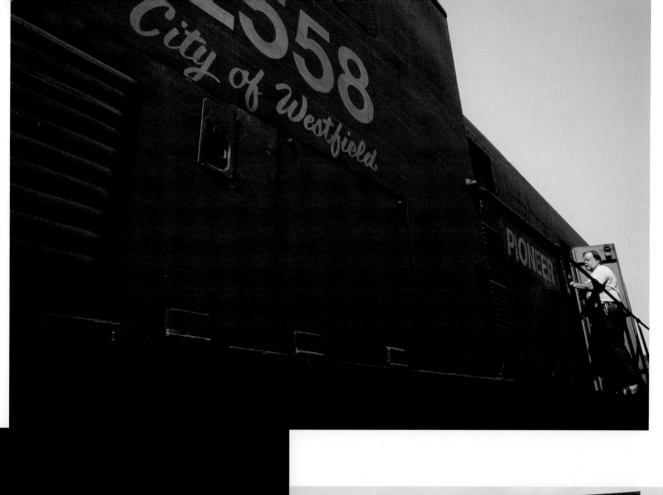

🎧 Sitting in the cab of GP38 No. 3802 on June 7, 2004, a Wisconsin & Southern engineer faces the setting sun as he runs toward Reedsburg, Wisconsin, on the old Chicago & North Western main line between Madison and St. Paul via Elroy. Once a double-track line with ABS protection, this remnant of the line is now just a single-track branch terminating at Reedsburg. Brian Solomon

A "6 brake" schedule on a Delaware-Lackawanna Alco-built RS-3. The top lever regulates the train air, and the bottom is the independent brake. This steam-era equipment was installed on many early diesels. The 6 brake was not self-lapping, and on reductions in brake-pipe pressure it required the engineer to lap the brake handle manually to fix the amount of air released. Brian Solomon

The engineer applies the independent brake with a swift, counterclockwise motion. Manipulating the air brake is a skill that is learned through practice. Brian Solomon

Upper: California Northern operates on track spun off by Southern Pacific in the mid-1990s. Engineer Tim Holbrook has his left hand on the independent brake and his right on the throttle as he switches freight cars with GP15-1 No. 108 at Corning, California, on July 7, 2005. He has depressed the independent brake handle to bail off the air. **Lower:** Tim Holbrook checks his paperwork before beginning his run on the former Southern Pacific West Valley Line. Traditionally the West Valley was the preferred route for SP passenger trains between the Bay Area and Oregon. Today, California Northern's daily local freights are the only traffic on the largely tangent line. Photos by Brian Solomon

Standing on the running boards of the locomotive, engineer Tim Holbrook starts his GP15-1 by priming the fuel pump. Brian Solomon

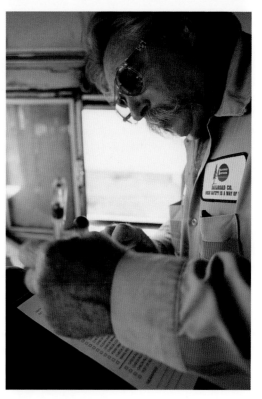

WORKING FREIGHT

Railroading in different environments requires various skills and many skill levels. Working a passenger train and keeping it on schedule to the minute on a busy multi-track railroad is a very different task than controlling a 15,000-ton, 150-car freight train in heavily graded territory. Neither is easy. The engineer of a short passenger train may need to bring his train from 79 mph (or faster) to a complete stop at a platform, often within inches of a specific point, while keeping the ride as smooth as possible for the comfort and safety of his passengers and to stay on schedule. A passenger engineer may be less concerned with the difficulties of starting his train on a grade and the risks to traction motors as the result of overheating, or the effects that his train handling has on train dynamics on a hogback grade.

Seaboard Coast Line's *Train Handling Instruction and Information Pertaining to Air Brake Equipment on Engines and Cars* is a 494-page document published in 1975 and designed to advise locomotive engineers on equipment and technique. The foreword explains, "Train dynamic behavior results from the interaction of numerous operating variables such as train handling procedures, train make-up, curvature, grade, speed, climate, etc. The proper handling of trains is absolutely necessary and required in the control of this interaction to avoid damage to the equipment, lading, and track structure." Later, the text articulates:

> *The twelve to fifteen thousand ton freight train, quite commonplace on many railroads today, is the product of many changes within the industry. . . . These longer, heavier, and faster trains have placed new demands on the knowledge and skills of the loco-motive engineman. There is strong evidence that an urgent need exists for upgrading train handling skills. Successful train handling requires an ability to start and stop the train and to control the slack action and speed while in motion through varying track gradients, curvatures, and speed zones, all without accident or damage.*

Continued from page 100

Safe train handling and proper use of the brake is one of the most difficult tasks in railroading. One of the great advantages of the railroad is its ability to move a great quantity of freight using a minimum of resources. Railroads have improved productivity by gradually increasing the amount of freight a single crew can handle. SCL's *Train Handling Instruction* dedicates a considerable portion of the text to the correct use of the air-brake system. It details how the braking system works, the differences among the types of equipment and braking throttle arrangements, how these react under various situations, and how they must be used correctly. For example, "One area of primary importance is that of minimum reduction. Modern locomotive equipment such as 26-L provides for a fixed minimum reduction. Previous equipment would permit almost any degree of brake pipe reduction under 6 or 8 psi." Later it states:

> *Train braking should be handled in a manner to provide flexibility in the control of train speed, slack action, and also to hold wheel damage and brake shoe wear to a minimum as well as reduce the dynamic forces between track and train.*
>
> *Under normal operating conditions, a brake application should begin at a sufficient distance so that desired retardation may be obtained by using an initial minimum service reduction. Normally, slowdowns or stops should be completed with not more than a 15 psi total brake pipe reduction. This will act to reduce train forces and also provide reserve braking, should conditions require that the train be stopped in a shorter distance than previously planned. The use of a full service leaves no reserve braking power (except an emergency brake application) and limits the engine-man's ability to control the train with the result that the stop point is dependent on the braking characteristics of the train. Proper train braking therefore requires planning ahead and the use of moderate brake pipe reductions.*

The dynamic brake is among the technologies afforded by the diesel-electric locomotive that greatly improved the operation of trains. The dynamic brake is a valuable tool for slowing and controlling long freight trains on a grade. SCL's *Train Handling Instruction* succinctly explains this technology:

The photographer captures a nocturnal interior view of Chicago & North Western General Electric Dash 9 No. 8615 at South Pekin, Illinois, in February 1996 as another train blitzes by on an adjacent track.
Steve Smedley

The dynamic brake is an electrical retarding device which utilizes the main generator and traction motors to retard the speed of the train. . . . [It] utilizes the energy of the train to turn the wheels of the locomotive against resistance of the motors, which are electrically converted to generators. The kinetic energy of the train is transformed into electrical energy which is dissipated by resistance grids on each locomotive unit. . . . The dynamic brake is, however, a brake of specifically limited capacity. This limit is the capability of the motors acting as generators to handle the voltage and current involved as well as the resistance grids and the blower fans to dissipate the energy without obtaining extreme conditions of amperage voltage and heat. The maximum dynamic horsepower capacity is proportionate to the number of traction motors on the locomotive and varies with locomotive model.

When starting a heavy train, an engineer has to be careful not to exert too much force too quickly lest he or she cause a "pull-apart" or overload damage to the traction motors (with traditional direct current traction locomotives). When descending grades, there are equivalent concerns. The engineer must carefully regulate his use of the various braking systems. When using the dynamic brake, the engineer must ensure he or she doesn't overload the motors. Since 1975, locomotive manufacturers General Electric and Electro-Motive Division have developed much more powerful and advanced machines. Microprocessor control, advanced fuel-injection systems, and improvements to traction-motor technology have contributed to more powerful, more fuel-efficient, and more sophisticated engines. Advancements have greatly improved the capabilities of dynamic braking too. Since computers now monitor, regulate, and control many aspects of locomotive operation, a modern-day General Electric Dash 9 typically used in heavy freight service is a much more sophisticated locomotive than a 1970s-era SD40-2. In addition to vastly improved fuel economy, power output, and braking power, it is much more difficult to accidentally damage these modern machines during the course of normal operation.

Operators' opinions on the new technology vary greatly. The reliable raw power and rapid loading of the SD40-2 has long been a favorite among those at the throttle. Yet, the new locomotives present numerous advantages for crews and operations. Working with locomotive engineers to make sure they understand and know how to use the new and evolving locomotive technology, while helping them master the skills needed to operate modern freight and passenger trains, is the role of a railroad's road foreman of engines. Travis Berryman is a road foreman of engines with BNSF Railway. He started out as a track laborer for the McCloud River Railroad in northern California and has enjoyed a variety of different positions with BNSF, including switchman in the busy Alliance Yard and later locomotive engineer in some demanding western terrain. He offers a perspective of working heavy freight in mountain territory where grades steeper than 2 percent are the norm. "Up here in the mountains it's extremely important to pay attention to the ammeter—both going up grade, and down

again in dynamic braking," he says. "The older units had short time ratings [on the motors] that you needed to watch. With the GE Dash 9s, if they exceed 1,300 amps, the engine will shut down [to prevent damage to the electric motors]."

When running in the mountains, Berryman stresses, "It's very important to know your territory; know where your rear end is, and know what's coming up 2 miles ahead. You need to know your surroundings, up hill, down hill, and around curves. You must know where you are at all times. Knowing where you are is more important than knowing your engines."

As a relatively young road foreman, Berryman explains that he often works with men years his senior who have more experience. "The engineers teach the foreman, and he teaches them," he says. Berryman has a positive perspective on the advantages of BNSF's GE Dash 9 fleet, stating "They are quieter, more comfortable, and more powerful [than the SD40-2s]. Since [GE] started making the Dash 9, they really have improved them. It's a damn good unit."

The trend in American railroading has been toward improved productivity, which has resulted in ever longer and heavier trains using as few employees as possible within the constraints of safe and reliable operation. In the last few years, some railroads have successfully employed distributed power units (DPU)—radio-controlled remote locomotive technology. Locomotives equipped with DPU can be placed anywhere in a train consist to overcome limitations imposed by curvature and drawbar weakness. These serve in a capacity similar to manned helpers working as rear-end or mid-train helpers. Throttle commands are transmitted to the remote units in a way that is similar to direct electrical multiple-unit connections, but allows for either individual or synchronized control of DPUs and it provides safety features in the event of a loss of radio contact. As a result, one engineer can individually operate a longer, heavier train in graded territory than possible with locomotives only at the head end.

Other advances are also being developed. Recently, Union Pacific announced it was investigating technology that may ultimately allow for safe operation of heavy freight with a single man in the cab.

🎧 **Upper:** In May 1999, Burlington Northern Santa Fe Kansas Division road foreman of engines Jerry Worchester (left) briefs the crew of the H-KCKBAR9 (Kansas City, Kansas–to–Barstow, California) train on the use of distributed power units (DPU)—radio controlled remote locomotives. This was one of the first BNSF manifest trains to work with DPU. **Lower:** BNSF engineer Mark Pierce, running BNSF Dash 9 No. 653, waves to the crew of a westward intermodal train as the two pass at speed on the former Santa Fe main line at Cassoday, Kansas, in 1999 parts. Photos by Dan Munson

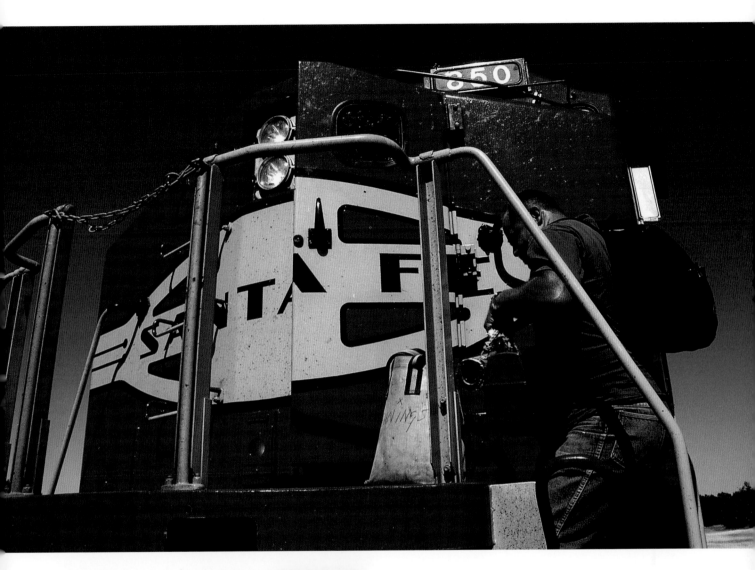

Engineer Denny Jackson boards Santa Fe Dash 8-40CW No. 850 with his travel grip for a trip west on train 787 from Ash Fork, Arizona, on June 13, 1993. Climbing the narrow stairs can be tricky while carrying an armload of groceries. Tom Kline

A view from the cab of Kansas City Southern coal train No. 98 is shown. The engineer of the opposing train (in the light-blue shirt) discusses logistics with the crew of No. 98 while stopped at the north siding switch of Gentry, Arkansas, on September 22, 2000. Tom Kline

Pictured is Canadian National's former Wisconsin Central Chicago Subdivision. The signal at Lost Arrow Road near Byron, Wisconsin, shows red, indicating "stop and proceed." Brian Solomon

CHAPTER

4

THE BIG PICTURE: LEVERMEN, OPERATORS, AND DISPATCHERS

*T*he weight and necessary speed of trains and the limitations of braking systems make it impractical to stop trains within sight distance. This fact, combined with trains' inability to pass and overtake one another except at preordained meeting places (where there are switches to access passing sidings, yards, or other running tracks), requires some method of authorizing train movements to avoid collisions, obtain maximum use of track space, and minimize delay.

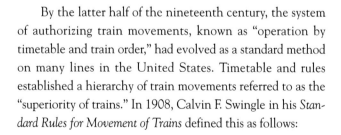

Maine Central's Beecher Falls local pauses at North Stratford, New Hampshire, in May 1955, illustrating a pace of life lost on modern Americans. The train order signal is "clear" in both directions, while a trainman has his feet up during a station stop. Note the marker lamps at the back of the combine. Jim Shaughnessy

In time-honored tradition, a Nickel Plate Road operator hands train orders to a westward manifest freight led by Berkshire-type No. 772 at North East, Pennsylvania. Jim Shaughnessy

By the latter half of the nineteenth century, the system of authorizing train movements, known as "operation by timetable and train order," had evolved as a standard method on many lines in the United States. Timetable and rules established a hierarchy of train movements referred to as the "superiority of trains." In 1908, Calvin F. Swingle in his *Standard Rules for Movement of Trains* defined this as follows:

A train is superior to another train by right, class or direction.

Right is conferred by train order; class and direction by timetable.

Right is superior to class or direction.

Direction is superior as between trains of the same class.

Swingle went on to specify, "Trains of the first class are superior to those of the second; trains of the second class are superior to those of the third; and so on."

It is crucial to understand that under the rules of the railroad, a "train" is a service, and not just a piece of equipment. The timetable used to operate a railroad is an official company document that authorizes train movements and should not be confused with the flyers issued to the public for their convenience. In the formative days of railroading, many companies relied on such official timetables to authorize train movements. For the timetable to work efficiently, trains must run on time. Keeping on schedule requires synchronized timekeeping, standardized time, and rigid adherence to the rules of the railroad. (Incidentally, prior to railroad timetables there was no standard time, so the American railroads invented it; later Railroad Standard time zones were adopted into general use.)

Railroads typically had a standard clock and required employees to use railroad-approved watches that needed to be inspected on a regular basis and regularly compared with a company clock. It was the responsibility of inferior trains to stay out of the way of superior trains per the timetable. Often this required inferior trains to be "in the clear"—on the siding—at least five minutes before the superior train was due past that point. Synchronized timing was crucial: if one conductor's watch was three minutes slow and the other's was three minutes fast, a collision might result.

Strict timetable operation is rigid and doesn't permit for the real-life variance of many railroad operations. Inevitably, some trains lose time and run late. When trains are late by a few minutes, it doesn't necessarily pose serious problems. The inferior trains, waiting in the clear as per the timetable, may only suffer a nominal delay. But delays can pile up, and after awhile the whole system starts to break down. Also, railroads often need to run extra trains—those not in the published timetable. The issuing of train orders, or "orders," modifies the published timetable for the special-purpose operations. An extra train may be added that runs on orders and thus, by definition, is superior to other trains. A late-running train may be advanced from one siding to another with orders, while other affected trains are advised of the change by train orders. The ability to amend timetables gave railroads flexibility when operating a single-track railroad. Late trains could be sped up to overtake slower trains in front of them and extra trains could be ordered to fill gaps in service as needed.

To make the system of train orders function, railroads stationed trained telegraph operators at strategic locations along the line. Typically, they worked in stations, interlocking towers, yards, and at places where remote sidings were routinely used to pass or meet trains. Telegraph operators, commonly known as "brass pounders," were fluent in the rapid clicks of coded dots and dashes transmitted over the wire, as developed by Samuel Morse and Alfred Vail. They were the eyes, ears, voice, and hands of a centralized dispatcher. In addition to copying and delivering orders, operators would also "os" (record times "on sheet") trains as they arrived, departed, or passed. The record was retained at the operator's station and the times were transmitted by telegraph to the dispatcher, who used them to keep tabs on the train's progress over the line.

Over the years, railroads developed a variety of different types of train orders—accompanied by detailed rules for their safe implementation—to cover almost every possible operating scenario. The rules for timetable and train-order operation filled many pages in the company rulebook. How did train orders work? After a lapse of time, if a time freight hadn't passed a station and the dispatcher wanted to advance a passenger train that was being delayed, he could wire orders to

At 1:55 p.m., operator Mike Barkoviak "os's" a train past the Bloomington, Illinois, BN target office—a one-story manual interlocking facility that protected the Norfolk Southern and Conrail diamond crossing with Southern Pacific's (former Gulf, Mobile & Ohio) line between Chicago and St. Louis. Steve Smedley

the operator and instruct the operator to lower his train-order signal—normally kept in the "clear" position—which let the train crew know they had to stop and collect orders. The dispatcher would then issue the orders, which were copied by the operator who transcribed the clicks coming over the wire. To ensure he had the instructions copied correctly, he repeated them verbatim over the wire for the dispatcher to confirm. The operator then produced a set of train orders for the train crews—written or typed on thin carbon paper known as "flimsies." Most railroads had two varieties of orders: "31 orders" that restricted the movement of the train and required a signature, and therefore required the train to stop to receive them, and "19 orders"

that either added authority or did not specifically restrict a train's existing authority, and thus could be taken "on the fly."

When it was necessary to deliver orders to a moving train, the operator attached the flimsies to a wooden cane with a hoop at one end and stood close to the tracks in position to hand them up as the train passed at speed. Usually he had two hoops; there was one for the head end and one for the conductor. An engineman—fireman or engineer, depending which side of the tracks the order station was on—snatched the hoop, quickly removed the orders, and dropped the hoop trackside for the operator to retrieve. In later years, many railroads used delivery hoops with a Y-shaped fork at one end, to which the orders were attached with string. Enginemen snatched the orders by ripping the string from the fork, but they didn't grab the whole hoop. The forked hoops saved the operator from having to walk the line to retrieve it. Such delivery was known as "hooping up orders." Some lines also used a fixed order delivery hoop with positions for several forks on which operators could hang orders. This arrangement did not require the operator to stand outside and wait for the train to pass.

Taking orders on the fly required a bit of nerve and dexterity. If the operator or train crew misjudged the hand-off, the train would have to stop to collect them. Depending on the stopping distance of a heavy freight or fast passenger train, this could result in a crewmember having to walk a half-mile or more, and harsh words might be exchanged if the operator was deemed at fault. Likewise, the operator needed to stand perilously close to the tracks at all times of day or night and in all weather to deliver orders. As the train roared past, he kept a sharp eye out for dragging equipment and other hazards because he might be the first victim if it was left unchecked.

Before a train could proceed on its schedule, it required a dispatcher's clearance card. The card indicated whether or not it had orders and was essentially a signal to proceed. Both timetable authority and dispatcher's orders were normally valid, until fulfilled, for up to 12 hours from the time of issue. If a train had not arrived at its destination within 12 hours of its orders, the orders were void and the authority to operate was withdrawn. At any time, a dispatcher could cancel an order or amend it with orders of a more restrictive type.

The telephone gradually superseded the use of the telegraph for transmitting orders to operators. Yet this transition was much slower than one might expect, and as late as the 1960s the telegraph was still preferred on some lines. When the telephone was used, strict lines of communication were established for the reading and copying of orders. The language of the train order was simple, direct, and very specific. When copying an order by phone, the dispatcher both said and spelled every number and named place to avoid confusion or mistakes. The operator read the order verbatim back to the dispatcher over the phone precisely as he copied it. When the dispatcher deemed it was correct, he confirmed it.

In later years, many railroads installed line-side phones at strategic points, such as at the ends of remote sidings. Crews could then communicate with operators, or in some situations directly with the dispatcher, who could advise them of delays or irregularities and provide additional information if required. (The large mazes of wires on poles once seen along railroad rights-of-way—now mostly gone—were due to all these telegraph, telephone, and signaling systems needed to run the railroad. Today, radio and buried fiber-optic data circuits have replaced these archaic technologies.)

Continued on page 116

Upper left: Delaware & Hudson operator Ken Sherman hands train orders to the *Laurentian* at XO Tower in Mechanicville, New York, in April 1970. **Left:** Running a Katy locomotive, the engineer of a Milwaukee Road northward freight bound for Bensenville, Illinois, snatches orders on the fly from the order post at Muscatine, Iowa, on January 30, 1985. Milwaukee Road commonly pooled power between Kansas City and Bensenville in the mid-1980s. Photos by Steve Smedley

113

In addition to delivering orders for the movement of trains, operators routinely handled other company business that was necessary for the movement of freight. The tower operator at Erie's MQ Tower at Campbell Hall, New York, hands waybills to a main line crew that made a pickup there on May 30, 1958. Jim Shaughnessy

On a cold day in January 1952, Delaware & Hudson freight RW-4 (Rouses Point, New York, to Wilkes-Barre, Pennsylvania) receives orders on the fly at Plattsburgh, New York. Jim Shaughnessy

Train orders allowed a dispatcher to amend the timetable. Orders were transmitted by telegraph or telephone to wayside operators who delivered them to trains. On November 25, 1956, the Burlington Route operator at Galva, Illinois, hands orders to the conductor of a westbound freight. Jim Shaughnessy

Montview operator Merle Sage hands orders to conductor J. C. Scruggs on southward freight No. 219, an Alexandria, Virginia–to–Atlanta, Georgia, intermodal train, at Lynchburg, Virginia's Montview Yard. Scruggs, now retired, was using a rolled-up flag to snare the orders. At the time the photo was made, trains changed crews at Monroe, Virginia, a small Amherst County railroad town 12 miles to the north. Following the Norfolk Southern merger, the entire operation at Monroe was closed and all functions were moved to Lynchburg. Doug Koontz

115

DISPATCHING BY TRAIN ORDER

Sitting at a desk with a large train sheet before him, a dispatcher authorized train movements and ensured his section of line was fluid. To do this effectively, he needed to calculate where and when trains would meet and draft the appropriate orders to transmit to operators for delivery, often hours in advance of the actual meets. Working as a dispatcher required detailed and expert knowledge of the line and operations. George S. Pitarys, who was an operator for Canadian Pacific and Maine Central before being promoted to train dispatcher on Maine Central, explains the thought process behind planning train orders: "Since you didn't have operators everywhere, you needed to project where to meet trains. You had to project running times, track speeds, keeping in mind the work that trains needed to do, and how different crews would respond. Once you made a meet, you were more or less stuck with it. If something fell down, it took extraordinary measures to change a meet if you didn't have operators in between."

The dispatcher had different types of orders that he could issue, depending on the circumstances. Some orders were absolute and gave a train authority to travel over a section of line between two points without restriction. Others were more flexible, and placed a degree of responsibility and decision making on train crews in the execution of the orders.

Continued from page 113

Such was the case with a typical "wait order," which included a time factor by which the order needed to be completed and after which it was no longer effective. Pitarys gives the example of an order he issued on the so-called Back Road of the Maine Central. The order was to a local freight with locomotive No. 562—an Electro-Motive GP7—that needed to work over several miles of track. The order also had to accommodate a through freight led by locomotive No. 402—a General Electric U18B—that needed to pass over the same territory. The written order read: "19 Order No. 54, June 8th 1984 to C&E Engine 562 at Danville Jct. Engine 402 run extra CP Royal Jct. to CP Oakland has right over extra 562 West CP Royal Jct. to Danville Jct. Wait at New Gloucester until 1:10 a.m. for Extra 562 West. Engine 562 run extra from Danville Jct. to CP Royal Jct. signed GSP."

MAINE CENTRAL RAILROAD COMPANY

FORM 19   FORM 19

TRAIN ORDER No. 54

June 8 19 84

TO C&E Eng 562   AT Danville Jct

X _____ OPR.; _____ M.

Eng 402 run Extra CP Royal Jct to CP Oakland
Has right over Extra 562 West
CP Royal Jct to Danville Jct
Wait at New Gloucester until 110 one ten AM
for Extra 562 West
Eng 562 run Extra Danville Jct to CP Royal Jct

Repeated At _____ 1153 P M.   Signed: _____ GSP
Employees addressed must each have a copy of this order.

Made *Com* time *1153 PM* *MacDonald*   Opr.

➲ This Maine Central 19 order was issued on June 8, 1984. Train orders such as this one were printed on flimsy carbon paper.
George S. Pitarys collection

This Maine Central 31 order was issued on June 8, 1984, to the conductor and engineman of Work Extra 563. In this situation, the train is an extra identified by the locomotive number. Notice that the order has a unique number, 56, and it indicates the time repeated back to the dispatcher.

George S. Pitarys collection

This would have been read over the phone to the operator at Danville Junction in the following manner:

Nineteen Order number fifty-four f-i-v-e f-o-u-r, to c and e engine 562 f-i-v-e s-i-x t-w-o at Danville Jct d-a-n-v-i double l-e j-c-t. Engine 402 f-o-u-r n-o-u-g-h-t t-w-o run extra CP Royal Jct r-o-y-a-l j-c-t to CP Oakland o-a-k-l-a-n-d- has right over extra 562 f-i-v-e s-i-x t-w-o West w-e-s-t CP Royal Jct r-o-y-a-l j-c-t to Danville Jct d-a-n-v-i double l-e j-c-t. Wait at New Gloucester n-e-w g-l-o-u-c-e-s-t-e-r until 1:10 o-n-e t-e-n a-m for Extra 562 f-i-v-e s-i-x t-w-o West w-e-s-t. Engine 562 f-i-v-e s-i-x t-w-o run extra from Danville Jct. d-a-n-v-i double l-e j-c-t to CP Royal Jct r-o-y-a-l j-c-t. signed GSP.

C&E referred to the conductor and enginemen. The order gave Extra 562 West until 1:10 a.m. to reach New Gloucester. If 562 West could not make it in time, it needed to remain in the clear at Danville Junction. The burden of making the meet safely was on the train crews. After 1:10, the 402 had permission to proceed without further contact with the dispatcher.

To the uninitiated, train orders look complicated, but for more than 100 years they were a standard method of dispatching trains in North America. Pitarys notes, "It took a lot of skill to dispatch trains with train orders. You really needed to think ahead and plan out your moves."

AUTOMATIC BLOCK SIGNALS

On busy lines, and on routes where railroads regularly operated multiple trains one right after another in one direction—typically on passenger lines—railroads installed automatic block signaling (ABS) to provide added protection. In its basic form, ABS was designed to give an added measure of protection for following moves. In some cases where ABS was employed, train crews were absolved from the need to protect the rear of their train when they fell behind schedule or made an unscheduled stop. Depending on the maximum speed of trains and the density of traffic, railroads could install two-, three-, or four-aspect block signals that respectively provided one, two, or three blocks' protection. The most common type of block signal displayed three aspects: red, amber (yellow), and green. These indicated "stop and proceed," "approach," and "clear," respectively.

Why did a red signal indicate "stop and proceed" and not a full and absolute stop? The assumption in ABS territory was that a red aspect reflected a shunted track circuit that could reflect the presence of a train in the block, an open switch, damage to the track, or simply a failed circuit. On most lines, ABS hardware displayed clear aspects unless the track circuit was shunted. By design, ABS signaling "failed safe," meaning if there was any flaw in the circuit or the equipment, the signals automatically displayed their most restrictive aspect. Since the signals operated automatically, there was no way for an engineer to know why the signal displayed a red aspect. Since signals were often at out-of-

the-way places, there was no way for him to communicate with a dispatcher or operator. Under the rules, a train could proceed past a "stop and proceed" indication at restricted speed (usually 10 to 20 mph and prepared to stop within one-half the sight distance) until it *passed* the next signal displaying a more favorable aspect. That way, if the signal displayed red as a result of a faulty track circuit, the train would not be unduly delayed. If there were a legitimate reason for the red aspect, the train would be able to stop short of obstruction. Generally speaking, since ABS only provided extra protection for following movements, these signals did *not* authorize train movements. A train operating on a line protected by ABS still required some kind of paper authority, which was usually granted by the timetable or train order. On lines with directional double track, trains can operate in accordance with rule 251, which authorizes movement on signal indication in the current of traffic. Yet, trains require authority to enter and exit 251 territory.

⊂ Pictured is Canadian National's former Wisconsin Central Chicago Subdivision. The signal at Lost Arrow Road near Byron, Wisconsin, shows red, indicating "stop and proceed." Brian Solomon

⊃ An eastward Guilford freight, lead by an SD45, passes a block signal east of Orange, Massachusetts, in February 2004. On the former Boston & Maine lines, twin-head intermediate block signals use a staggered arrangement and feature a distinct number plate to distinguish them from home signals. This signal had displayed a green-over-red aspect (clear), which turned to red-over-red when the train shunted the track circuit. Brian Solomon

TOWERS AND INTERLOCKINGS

At busy junctions and on lines with multiple track (two or more main tracks), railroads built interlocking towers to control the movement of trains. Here, levermen and operators worked to keep the railroad fluid. To prevent the accidental lining of conflicting routes, signals and switches were interlocked mechanically (and in later years, electrically). Interlockings are designed to make it impossible to accidentally line up two routes through a plant that allows for conflicting movements. This is reliant, of course, on enginemen obeying the signals.

Rules governing interlocking movements granted operating authority on signal indication. Unlike automatic block signals, which were "permissive," interlocking signals were "absolute." A red aspect at an interlocking signal was a full "stop" that could not be passed without explicit permission from the tower operator or dispatcher controlling it. To avoid confusion, railroads ensured that ABS and interlocking signals had sufficiently different appearances and identification.

On many multiple-track lines, towers passed trains from one interlocking to the next. Towers communicated with one another as to the occupancy of track and line routes, and to clear the appropriate signals. Often tracks could be used to move trains in either direction depending on prevailing traffic and agreement between towers. Typically towers were under the authority of the dispatcher, but were often granted a measure of autonomy. Operation using towers offered a degree of operational flexibility, facilitated faster trains to overtake slower ones, and allowed for the maximum use of track space. This system increased capacity, minimized delays, and kept the line fluid while maintaining a high level of safety. As a dispatcher on a large western railroad explains, "Fluidity is the key to a well-run railroad. Once fluidity is let go to fulfill other priorities, the railroad begins to congeal."

Let's take a look at operations in the early 1990s on the former New York Central multiple-track line into Grand Central Terminal, now on Metro-North. There were situated key points where tower directors, operators, levermen, and signal maintainers worked to keep the line fluid. The number of people required in a tower depended on its size and workload. Much of the line involved four main tracks and sets of universal crossovers (allowing the movement from any main track to any other in both directions) to keep a continuous

The tower director is pictured at Chicago Union Station tower on July 24, 1964. At busy towers, several employees are required to keep pace with the demands of traffic. A tower director handles big-picture route planning and calls out moves to levermen or operators. John Gruber

control current of traffic on the four main tracks between towers. Above each switch lever was a corresponding switch number that lit when the switch was unlocked. When the operator cleared a signal, a light illuminated the signal number while the respective switch lights went out to provide confirmation that the route was properly lined. The tower controlled three sets of home signals—absolutes—arranged on bridges at 110th Street, at the tower at 106th Street, and at 102nd Street.

flow of passenger trains moving. At peak times, dozens of trains each hour carried tens of thousands of commuters between the New York City suburbs and Manhattan along former New York Central and New Haven routes.

Jay Grumblatt was an operator at "Nick" Tower, which straddled the four-track main at 106th Street. It was located between 125th Street Station and the entrance to the Park Avenue Tunnel at 97th Street, on the approach to Grand Central. In telegraph days, towers typically had a one- or two-letter designation for easy and distinctive identification. In those days, this tower was known as "NK." Following the creation of Conrail in 1976, the tower was changed to "Nick" to avoid confusion with another NK tower elsewhere on the system. Grumblatt reminisces, "Nick was a penthouse in Harlem. It was a really wonderful place with windows every which way. You could see a train coming a long way out."

Nick controlled the line from the 138th Street Bridge over the Harlem River to about 60th Street in the Park Avenue Tunnel. The operator worked an old General Railway Signal Co. frame with 44 levers operated with formed handles similar to pistol grips. He used a trigger to unlock them, and pulled them in and out to line switches and clear signals. Grumblatt recalls there were 12 levers to line-and-lock the crossovers, 24 to clear signals, and 8 traffic levers to

In the evening rush, track Nos. 1, 3, and 4 were used for outbound moves, and the No. 2 track was used for inbound moves. The operator at Nick received advance warning of approaching trains from towers on either side. To the north (New York Central direction West) was MO Tower at Mott Haven, the junction between the Hudson and Harlem Lines, and in New York Central days the location of an enormous coach yard for making up and storing trains. To the south were various towers in Grand Central Terminal itself, including A, B, C, and U towers. If everything was running normally, Nick lined trains through the plant according to a preplanned program based on the timetable. When a southward (inbound) train passed MO, the operator there would "os" the move on the open-phone wire. For example, "1577 south from MO to U on two," and the operator at Nick got an approach light on his board when 1577 reached 125th Street. By this time, he could physically see the train and should have cleared the signals on No. 2 track in the southward direction. If he did this in a timely fashion, the train would see green aspects all the way through the plant. However, if trains were running late and the program had fallen apart, the dispatcher could instruct the operator at

Nick to line trains though the crossovers and move them from one track to another. This move might be done to get a late-running express around an all-stops local.

One of the busiest towers on the line was Tower A in Grand Central, located at the throat of the terminal where tracks fanned out to reach the upper-level platforms. The complexity of the plant and intensity of traffic required a yardmaster, tower director, operator, and three levermen. The director called out the moves to the levermen who physically worked the levers, while the operator recorded the passage of trains and kept the director informed of train movements. Grumblatt recalls the work of a leverman here: "This was one of the toughest jobs. You were constantly on your feet. The director would call out the moves and you might have to move as many as 20 levers to make it."

Continued on page 125

↟ Operator Dan Kopak works Conrail's BEND Tower at South Bend, Indiana, in July 1996. Note the pistol-grip levers at right. BEND controlled Conrail's busy former New York Central Chicago Line and the crossing with Canadian National's former Grand Trunk Western Chicago and Battle Creek main line. The tower was closed in early 1997 after the two double-track lines were separated along their joint right-of-way and a more direct crossing was built west of BEND. Pete Ruesch

➲ A characteristic image of a tower operator is shown. Dan Kopak works in the bay window of BEND Tower in June 1996 as a Conrail GE Dash 8-40CW rolls past the window. The train sheet was used for keeping a record of train movements. Pete Ruesch

CSX operator Jim Vargo gives Amtrak No. 30, the *Capitol Limited*, the roll-by at R Miller Tower, West Virginia. Checking to see if passing trains were in good order was an important part of an operator's duty. Doug Koontz

Operator Jay Grumblatt works Metro-North's "Nick" Tower on July 7, 1993. This classic tower straddled the old New York Central main line to Grand Central at 106th Street in Manhattan. Joe Geronimo

Carl Scharf, a leverman/operator at Metro-North's C Tower in Grand Central Terminal, is shown on April 14, 1993. In the 1990s, Metro-North phased out its remaining towers in favor of a centralized dispatching center based in Grand Central. Joe Geronimo

An operator gives a roll-by as a Burlington Northern freight crosses the Milwaukee Road at Mendota Tower, Illinois, on August 18, 1978. John Leopard

Above: An operator works the "armstrong" levers at Mendota Tower, Illinois, on August 18, 1978. **Right:** Note the Burlington Northern train orders above the operator and track panel on left at BN's Mendota Tower, Illinois.
Photos by John Leopard

Continued from page 122

CENTRALIZED TRAFFIC CONTROL

Traditionally, the extent of territory controlled by a tower was dictated by the physical limitations of mechanical signaling and interlocking machinery. Controlling signals and points with a mechanical pipeline allows a single tower to control signals and points over 1 or 2 miles of track at most. With the advent of new technologies, control was expanded. Electro-mechanical, electropneumatic, and all-electric plants greatly enlarged what an individual leverman/operator could work effectively. Using these technologies, railroads combined the functions of smaller towers into larger, centrally located control centers.

By 1911, the development of complex electrical relay circuits had led to the invention of Absolute Permissive Block signaling (APB). This automatic system was used to greatly improve capacity of single-track lines while maintaining a high level of safety. It still required a traditional method of authorizing train movements—typically timetable and train-order rules. APB technology, largely the work of General Railway Signal's Sedgwick N. Wight, was advanced in the 1920s to produce Centralized Traffic Control (CTC). Today, this is considered one of the great labor-saving technologies of the twentieth century in any industry. In its original form, CTC signaling used relay circuits and automatic signals over a section of line, and effectively blended interlocking rules with the principles of operation offered by automatic block and APB signaling.

With CTC, an operator could control home signals over a much longer section of line than had been possible with earlier types of interlocking equipment. An operator from a centralized location could remotely clear electrically controlled wayside signals. Relay circuits provided a fail-safe electric interlocking mechanism that was designed to prevent the operator from accidentally lining conflicting moves, or simultaneously directing two trains over the same section of track.

This was a radical change. With CTC, wayside home signals were used to authorize train movements, which dispensed with the need for timetable and train-order rules. Track circuitry was used to automatically "os" trains; this information was displayed using lights on a panel in front of the operator. Although not specifically required by CTC, most installations also gave the operator control of track switches. A CTC operator could line up meets and direct the flow of traffic over the line without the need to work through intermediaries. Furthermore, he could see the position of every train on his railroad at a glance and watch as trains progressed over the line. CTC greatly increased line capacity, improved safety, and lowered operating costs, since it no longer required numerous trackside operators to copy and deliver orders. On the downside, CTC was extremely costly to install and expensive to maintain.

Among the first CTC installations were relatively short sections of line on New York Central and Boston & Maine, where CTC had increased the capacities of very busy lines that carried a mix of freight and passenger traffic. CTC's flexibility increased fluidity, and as the technology was refined more railroads adopted it for heavily traveled lines. Railroads such as Western Pacific used

On October 22, 1955, Boston & Maine tower operator (train director) R. P. Fonda works the JV Tower at Johnsonville, New York, where lines to Troy and Mechanicville, New York, split. Long closed, the gutted remains of this tower still stand today as a ghostly reminder of Johnsonville's past importance to the railroad. Johnsonville is now just a wide place along Guilford's remaining east-west main line. *Jim Shaughnessy*

Large, complex CTC installations not only allowed railroads to close operators' stations but they consolidated the functions of towers, too. A tower was no longer needed to operate a set of crossovers or to control a grade-level crossing with another railroad. These functions could easily be moved to a remote CTC board. Likewise, as CTC sections became larger, the task of working the CTC machines was transferred from operators directly to dispatchers.

The development of even more advanced computer systems has allowed for the melding of modern computer technology with CTC operation. Control of track sections has moved from traditional CTC boards to the computer screen. Instead of lining switches and clearing signals using knobs and switches on a panel, a dispatcher now controls them with a keyboard or mouse. Train data that was once recorded on traditional train sheets is now logged and recorded by computers. Dispatchers have gradually assumed not only the duties of the levermen and operators, but also of clerks and yardmasters.

A modern dispatching console uses computer screens to display a track model that shows track occupancy, conditions of signals and switches, and more detailed information like train direction. Identification tags may indicate train symbol, leading locomotives, and details such as the weight and length of a train, in addition to train direction. These tags follow the progress of a train across a district and make it possible to prioritize trains. Dispatchers can line a variety of moves in advance and cancel them if conditions change. In addition, with the most advanced systems, computers can run programs that plan and line meets based on train speeds and scheduling priorities. Checks within the software prevent conflicting moves and avert the possibility that human error will cause an accident. Not surprisingly, computers have increased the amount of territory assigned to individual dispatchers

On August 7, 1991, Don Larson, a dispatcher on Cyprus Northshore Mining at Silver Bay, Minnesota, works a classic CTC board to authorize train movements, while using a train sheet to log train activity. The top two rows of switches were used to line the points of track switches and to clear signals. Switches controlling points could be set for "normal" or "reverse." Signals used were cleared with three-position switches. John Leopard

CTC on long sections of main lines to eliminate operators and speed the flow of traffic. WP operated hundreds of miles of remote trackage across the western desert and Sierra Nevada range. Instead of waiting hours on remote sidings to fulfill train-order meets, trains were advanced by CTC to the most efficient meeting places. By the late 1950s, railroads, especially in the East, were suffering from a dramatic drop in traffic levels. CTC was installed as a cost-cutting measure and replaced traditional directional double-track main lines with a single main track and passing sidings. This line arrangement was often more effective for running the heavy, longer freight trains that were made possible by modern diesel-electric locomotives.

TRACK WARRANTS AND DIRECT TRAFFIC CONTROL

Due to the high cost of implementation, railroads only invest in CTC where it will produce the best return; CTC has generally not been applied to lightly traveled main lines, branches, and secondary routes. Instead, other forms of track authorization are used. Advances in radio technology during the 1960s, 1970s, and 1980s allowed for the gradual phasing out of traditional means of granting authority, such as timetable and train-order rules, and some forms of manual blocks. Fewer train-order stations were required and eventually methods for delivering the orders over the radio were implemented. Strict forms of communication were developed to allow train crews to copy orders over the radio. During an interim period, some lines used dispatchers to relay train orders to operators by phone. The operators then delivered the orders either by flimsies or, increasingly, by radio.

By the mid-1980s, few railroads were operating scheduled passenger trains anymore and the majority of freights were being operated as extras. Modern radio communications had been fully implemented, virtually all locomotives had cab radios, and most employees were equipped with rugged portable sets. During this time, most railroads dispensed with traditional timetable and train-order rules altogether. All trains were effectively operated as "extras," and new systems were devised to grant track authority using radio delivery. These systems allow the direct communication between dispatcher and train crews, and permit the dispatcher to authorize train movements without the need for intermediaries. Like train orders, these new systems employ forms relaying simple, direct, and very specific information. On receiving an authority over the radio, a crew must repeat it verbatim to the dispatcher, who must confirm it as correct before it can be implemented. Dispatchers must keep carefully written records of track authority granted and the records must correspond exactly with the authority issued to trains. Likewise, train crews keep written records of authority issued to them.

Computer systems are often used to assist dispatchers in issuing track authority and to avoid issuing duplicate or overlapping authority. Railroad rules require verbal transmissions to be recorded so that all communication between dispatcher and crews can be reviewed in the event of an accident.

Several different systems are used in the United States, including direct traffic control (DTC), track warrant control (TWC), and The Form D Control System (DCS) used under the Northeast Operation Rules Advisory Committee (NORAC). The TWC and DCS systems are similar to the old train-order system and use flexible limits that may be tailored by milepost or designated control point to match the needs of specific train movements. DTC limits are defined strictly by blocks and can be compared to the system of manual block.

⊃ Delaware-Lackawanna conductor Shawn Palermo completes Form D paperwork during the run over Pocono Summit. Brian Solomon

THE TRAIN DISPATCHER

In the context of modern operations, the train dispatcher is the most essential position in railroading. Without a dispatcher's authority, nothing moves and the tracks cannot be maintained. The railroad is essentially frozen. In 1908, Calvin F. Swingle described the position as follows:

> Train dispatchers are almost invariably promoted from the ranks of operators entitled to promotion. The duties of a train dispatcher require him to be possessed of a fair knowledge of the working of the operating department of a railroad, and adept at figures, and should have a keen foresight, so he quickly and correctly executes a number of moves ahead and provides for that which may not work just as anticipated.
>
> [The dispatcher] should endeavor to get the ideas of his superiors so fixed in his mind that when left to his own resources he may act properly and in accordance with their wishes. He should be governed by the instructions of those in authority and never encourage or conceal any violations of rules by others. He should not allow a desire for the popularity among those in the train or telegraph service to influence him in any way and should show no partiality.

Swingle also wrote, "There is a constant strain on the nerves of a train dispatcher, on which account his hours of duty are generally short."

Many things have changed, but some of these descriptions of the dispatcher's job remain valid. The dispatcher's job has some of the most restrictive hours under the Federal Hours of Service Act. Where train crews are limited to 12 hours, dispatchers are limited to just 9 hours, and are typically scheduled to work 8 hours on a shift.

On many railroads, the training of dispatchers has fundamentally changed as a result of the virtual elimination of the traditional positions from which a dispatcher was promoted. Wayside operators and interlocking towers have been largely replaced by technology. The clerks who handled the paperwork at locations around the system have been eliminated by automatic car readers and centralized computer systems. Traditionally, a dispatcher could have only attained promotion after years of working the ground. Today, many freight railroads hire candidates for dispatching off the street. Like the modern conductor, the dispatcher's position is often an entry-level railroad job. Some lines view the dispatcher's position as management training rather than as a career itself.

Now it isn't possible for dispatcher candidates to learn the railroad the old-fashioned way. Instead, the railroads provide intensive classroom training over a period of months, followed by some field experience and a period of on-the-job training under the tutelage of an experienced dispatcher.

There are exceptions. Marshall Beecher has worked both as a tower operator and dispatcher for Chicago's Metra, a regional suburban passenger service operator. He explains that, as of 2005, Metra still operated eight towers and dispatchers were normally promoted from tower operators. In his view, "Working as a tower operator is much more real. You see the moves that you make, which makes it easier to expedite train movements. Your trains are more than just a lit track circuit. There's nothing like being there to look out the window."

Jay Grumblatt, who worked on New York's Metro-North during the transition from a tower-operated railroad to a centralized dispatched line, explains that the railroad is now run with 11 dispatcher desks based in Grand Central Terminal: "Things are as efficient now [as they were] with the towers. Today, you have the big picture. You can see from one end of the railroad to the other. You see the condition of every track circuit and you know where each train is. In the past, you could watch trains pass an interlocking, but between them you couldn't see where the trains were."

Dispatchers on the large freight railroads typically work huge centralized dispatching centers that employ hundreds of people and control tens of thousands of track miles. CSX's dispatching center is at Jacksonville, Florida; Union Pacific's is at Omaha, Nebraska; and

BNSF Railway's is at Fort Worth, Texas. Norfolk Southern still uses more moderately sized regional centers. Sitting at a desk and working from a computer console with phones and a radio transmitter, a dispatcher authorizes train movements to direct the flow of traffic over a defined line section, often described as a "district" or a "desk." The types of territory vary: maybe a linear portion of main line, a complex terminal area, or a group of disconnected secondary or branch lines. The types of track authorization are dependent on the hardware in place on the ground, the density of traffic, and the railroad's rules. Dispatching all districts from one centralized office has a variety of benefits. Dispatchers from adjoining districts can see what the others are doing and thus be better prepared for trains crossing from one territory to another. Railroad managers have greater flexibility in assigning dispatching jobs, while traffic managers and decision makers can quickly see how the railroad is performing and have specific train data available at a moment's notice.

● Norfolk Southern Piedmont Division dispatchers work a modern computerized dispatching center at Greenville, South Carolina, in late 1994. The dispatchers sit at computer consoles with large illuminated track diagrams positioned in a semicircle beyond. Unlike other large systems, NS has not moved toward one unified dispatching center to control the entire railroad. Doug Koontz

◖ Frank Suddeth works the south-end board at Southern Railway's Piedmont Division dispatching office at Greenville, South Carolina. This board handled trackage between Atlanta, Georgia, and Greenville, South Carolina. Four dispatchers worked out of this office and used three different systems for allocating track authority: two worked "dark territory" using a train sheet, and one was dispatched with a 1970s-era computer system. The position pictured here used a General Railway Signal relay-style console. All were replaced by a state-of-the-art computerized dispatch center in the early 1990s. Doug Koontz

Continued on page 133

CHICAGOLAND OPERATOR AND DISPATCHER

By Ed King

I answered an ad in the *Chicago Tribune* from the Milwaukee Road seeking tower operators in the Chicago area, and went to work for them in 1983.

As I qualified at Tower A5 (Pacific Junction), where the West Sub (the Elgin–Savanna route) and the C&M Sub (Chicago & Milwaukee) to Milwaukee divided; Tower B12 at Franklin Park, situated at the Soo Line crossing at the east end of Bensenville Yard; Tower B17 at the west end of Bensenville; Spaulding, where the Elgin, Joliet & Eastern crossed, east of the Fox River; and Rondout (the famous tower on the Milwaukee line where the Fox Lake commuter line joined and the EJ&E was crossed again. Towers B12, B17, and Spaulding were all on the Elgin Sub; Rondout was on the C&M.

As an extra operator, I worked all three shifts at all these towers. Tower B17 was the busiest. Not only did you have the commuter rushes and some yard moves, but also the above-mentioned business with the Chicago & North Western trying to handle Milwaukee Road freights in and out. Copying train orders for both dispatchers added to the load.

Tower A5 was quite busy, too. It was necessary to handle the commuter rushes through the junction. Inbound in the morning, this wasn't a big problem. You just ran them as they came. Trains from the Elgin Sub were crossed over from No. 2 main west of the tower and operated on No. 3 main downtown. You could thus handle two inbound "scoots" at the same time—a Fox Lake train straight through on No. 2 and the Elgin on No. 3. Outbound was another matter; you had to keep track, and make sure the Elgins didn't go to Rondout, and vice versa. The A5 and Rondout had to handle the Amtrak Milwaukee–Chicago

trains (the Hiawatha service) as well as train Nos. 7 and 8, the Empire Builder.

A5 was not without its little satisfactions. One fine day No. 8 was late and the best information had it passing by A5 right in the middle of the outbound rush. But No. 8 got by Mayfair (the C&NW tower 3.6 miles north of A5) and things were looking good. I had an Elgin scoot clearing the tower and the next outbound was a Fox Lake man followed closely by another Elgin scoot. I got the first Elgin out of the way and gave No. 8 the signal. He went by the tower at about 70 mph as the Fox Lake train went west. He never got a yellow, and neither did the second Elgin train. You weren't always that lucky.

I liked the autonomy and the responsibility of the towers. I enjoyed the work with the train crews, dispatchers, and yard folks. There were comfortable routines in all of them, and dispatchers' phones and radios meant you were never really alone. Spaulding was closed while I worked the towers, and its plants were moved to B17. That added to the load there, but not to excess. Indeed, it was often easier, because you had more timely knowledge of where the trains were and more notice of when they'd possibly interfere with the smooth flow of traffic. Lining switches and signals for the various moves was always interesting. Snowy weather and icing conditions often meant that signal maintainers and section laborers would have to help keep everything working, even for plants equipped with switch heaters.

I qualified as a dispatcher in 1984. There were three dispatchers' desks in Chicago Union Station

(Room 210). The C&M desk handled the 85.7 miles from Chicago to Milwaukee and the 17.2-mile Fox Lake Sub. The North Line suburban trains turned left at Rondout on their way to Fox Lake. The C&M dispatcher had a big General Railway Signal (as I recall) console machine that handled the double-track CTC from Morton Grove (just north of Mayfair) to KK Bridge at Milwaukee, 69.1 miles (except for the small gap at Rondout and another at Sturtevant, where a local operator controlled the crossovers in the vicinity). At the time I qualified, the C&M dispatcher also handled the 121.3 miles from Bensenville to Savanna—the Elgin and D&I Subdivisions—with train orders.

One would think that on the hottest main line of a railroad noted for speed, like the Milwaukee, that the switches and crossovers would be capable of high-speed operation, but not so. The C&M CTC controlled double crossovers in high-speed territory at Morton Grove (milepost 14.3), Tower A20 (milepost 20.5), Deerfield (milepost 24.2), Wadsworth (milepost 42.9), and Lake (milepost 77.2). All were 25 mph except those at Deerfield, which were good for 40 mph. The crossovers handled by the plants at Rondout and Sturtevant (milepost 61.8) were also 25 mph. This meant that if you had to mix fast traffic and slow, moves had to be planned carefully to avoid undue delays. You really didn't want to put a 120-car drag through a 25-mph crossover if you could help it. Amtrak trains and scoots could get through these crossovers and get back up to speed quickly. The

C&M dispatcher had to plan things carefully in order to earn a bonus from Amtrak for on-time performance. Usually, we got those bonuses, but they consisted of a plaque and a cap or jacket in lieu of a raise.

The Iowa desk handled the Dubuque Sub from the junction with the Milwaukee–Twin Cities main line at LaCrescent, Minnesota (opposite LaCrosse, Wisconsin), down the west side of the Mississippi River through Sabula Junction (across the river from Savanna), 160.1 miles (crews changed at Dubuque), and the Davenport Sub from Savanna through Sabula Junction to Muscatine, 81.9 miles. This included trackage rights over the "Dry Line" (the Davenport Rock Island & North Western) between Clinton and West Davenport (35.6 miles). It was operated by train orders between LaCrescent and Sabula, and track warrants from there to Muscatine (milepost 220.2). It was later changed to track warrants for the whole distance and took over the line from Elgin to Savanna when that was converted to track warrants a couple of years after I qualified.

The third desk was the Missouri desk, which took over where the Iowa desk left off at Muscatine and handled to Polo, the junction with the C&NW Des Moines–Kansas City line, and on to Kansas City, specifically Knoche Yard, which was shared under trackage rights with the Kansas City Southern, a total of 279.8 miles.

I had mixed emotions about the transfer from train-order operation to track warrants. Train orders were, in my opinion, much safer. Being transmitted to an operator for delivery to a train and conforming to very stringent forms prescribed by the rules provided checks against mistakes not available with track warrants, which were transmitted directly to the trains. One of the old-time dispatchers who qualified me on the Iowa desk called them "death warrants." Of course, track warrants saved money—line-of-road operators handling train orders were no longer necessary.

Ed King is pictured working as a Canadian Pacific dispatcher at Chicago Union Station, a few days before the dispatching desks were moved to Minneapolis. Ed stayed in the Chicago area for a few more months and worked at Rondout Tower before retiring to Florida. *John Gruber*

Belt Railway of Chicago dispatcher John Campbell works the desk at Clearing Yard. In the 1990s, BRC replaced an older dispatching station with a state-of-the-art, computer-aided system, but left the old CTC panels in place as a visual aid for dispatchers. At the time of this photograph on July 2, 1995, BRC's 28 miles of main line were handling more than 200 moves daily. Brian Solomon

Continued from page 129

On the downside, train dispatchers are generally insulated from the railroad environment and are often hundreds, sometime thousands, of miles from their territory. Too often, a train is little more than a dot on a computer screen. In these situations, it can be difficult to be empathetic with what is actually happening on the ground. It could even result in reduced efficiency and possibly reduced safety.

Many of the changes since the days of timetable and train-order authority have resulted in an increased burden on the individual train dispatcher. For example, when using traditional methods, a dispatcher had several ways of assigning responsibility to people on the ground. He could deliver a wait order, as described earlier, which placed the burden of responsibility on the train crews to complete the order. The decision of whether the train advanced to the next meeting point or remained where it had been was up to the crew—provided they executed the order within the time allotted. Maintenance forces, track inspectors, and others who needed access to the tracks were accommodated by issuing train lineups at regular intervals. These lineups listed trains ordered over the line, the departure from their respective terminals, and recent times past established operating points. Work crews then had knowledge of when trains were expected and, depending on the nature of the work, they could access the line without obtaining specific track authorization from the dispatcher. It was up to them to stay out of the way of trains. Towers along the line executed dispatcher instructions and facilitated normal moves over the line without the need to involve the dispatcher with the details. The ability to differentiate responsibility freed the dispatcher for other tasks such as big-picture planning. A dispatcher had more time to work out the flow of traffic, not just in the immediate minutes before setting up a meet but hours down the line.

↻ On the night of September 8, 1996, regular operator Brenda Bob (foreground, right) trains new operator Marcus Phillips (beyond) in the complexities of Southern Pacific's Tower 68 at Englewood Yard in Houston, Texas. To manage the activity, they view seven computer screens—six of which display track diagrams—in order to maintain smooth movements in and out of this major yard. Tom Kline

On the other hand, with most of today's lines, the dispatcher is directly responsible for authorizing all aspects of track authority and overseeing the details related to the execution of his orders. Everyone—trains, track maintenance forces, and others—must work through the dispatcher to obtain access to the tracks. Specific authority to occupy track is now required and the vagaries of wait orders are no longer acceptable. The reason for this is simple: to maintain a higher level of safety, it is now deemed necessary to channel all track access through a central authority—the dispatcher. As one dispatcher explained, "The old system of issuing track car lineups was inherently unsafe."

The goals of safety and operating efficiency are often at odds—the safest railroad is one that runs no trains. Focusing all aspects of granting track authority on the dispatcher has greatly increased his or her workload, and a dispatcher is already burdened by a host of clerical responsibilities that were once handled by the operators, clerks, and yardmasters. A dispatcher on a busy line complained that he routinely takes more than 200 phone calls in an eight-hour shift.

To help the dispatcher, railroads use the computer-aided systems described earlier to assist with facilitating the lining of switches and clearing of routes. Using computerized systems frees a dispatcher from some of the work involved with making meets. Instead of having to physically set each set of points and line individual home signals along the way, the dispatcher can highlight the route for a train and let the machine take care of the details. Furthermore, a well-designed system can automatically calculate where to meet trains, line switches behind, and set up the next route without minute-by-minute attention from the dispatcher. Automated safety checks that follow interlocking principles avoid the potential of conflicting movements.

Not all computer systems have achieved the same degree of efficiency, however. The success of computer-assisted dispatching systems is dependent on the quality of the computer software and hardware. It also depends on the nature of specific railroad operation, the amount of territory assigned to an individual dispatcher, the intensity and variety of train movements, how the authority is granted (CTC, DTC, or TWC), the type and degree of dispatcher training, and the level of extraneous clerical work imposed. In some areas, modern dispatching techniques have been very successful, but in others they have resulted in chaos. When the dispatcher becomes overloaded, the railroad grinds to a halt.

This view of A2 Tower in Chicago on June 18, 2004, shows the Daily Train Activities sheet, with the tower director out of focus beyond. The Daily Train Activities sheet is the program that the director uses to work. Metra employs both a director and leverman at A2. The two positions are required to handle the great volume of traffic; the director is the brains, the leverman is the hands. Brian Solomon

Operator Clarence Mild is a leverman at A2 Tower, Chicago. Located northwest of Chicago Union Station, A2 controls movements at the busy junction between passenger lines out of both Union Station and North Western Terminal. Although built by Milwaukee Road, it followed Pennsylvania Railroad specifications because Milwaukee used PRR's "Panhandle" route to reach Union Station. As built in 1938, this machine featured an 83-lever interlocking.
Brian Solomon

Clarence Mild works the frame at Chicago's A2 Tower. This is a rare surviving example of a Union Switch & Signal Model-14 electropneumatic interlocking. A horizontal, mechanical interlocking bed prevents the lining of conflicting moves.
Brian Solomon

Tower director Henry Thigpen works A2 Tower, Chicago. A few towers have survived in the Chicago area because of the complexity of operations and heavy volume of traffic there. Towers also serve as valuable training facilities for dispatchers. Brian Solomon

Operator Jim Wall works the interlocking machine at Metra's 67th Street Tower in Chicago. The large pistol levers in this former Illinois Central facility pull in and out to line switches and clear signals. Since this tower's heyday on IC's legendary eight-track main line, many levers have been removed or painted white to indicate they are out of service. The circular glass devices above the levers are time locks. Notice that the freight tracks have been blanked out of the diagram because movements over these tracks are no longer controlled by 67th Street. Brian Solomon

⌒ **Upper:** Shown is Burlington Northern Santa Fe's Marceline dispatcher desk at Kansas City, Kansas, on May 8, 2003.
Lower: On September 1, 1996, at Southern Pacific's Tower 17 in Rosenberg, Texas, clerk/operator Paul Garza talks on the phone about train consists that he's building to serve local shippers. Garza spent 20 years working in this ancient tower. Built in 1903, it still used the old pistol-grip interlocking machine on the left. The tower has since closed and was moved several blocks away to the town's railroad museum. Photos by Tom Kline

⊃ At Burlington Northern Santa Fe's massive Network Operations Center at Fort Worth, Texas, in April 1999, display screens provide up-to-date information on various traffic sectors.
Dan Munson

🎧 On February 24, 1988, a Conrail track worker welds the diamond in Palmer, Massachusetts, to build up material in the frog for grinding into shape, as a Central Vermont GP9 waits in the distance. Diamonds require constant maintenance.
Brian Solomon

CHAPTER

5

WORKING ON THE RAILROAD (LITERALLY): MAINTENANCE

*T*he rugged appearance of railroad tracks gives an illusion of permanence, yet the repair and maintenance of railroad rights-of-way and tracks are never-ending processes. Railroad track structure serves several crucial functions. Tracks provide a running surface for trains, and as a continuous fixed guide they must adequately distribute the weight of passing trains while guiding their wheels through every inch of the journey. The right-of-way serves as drainage to keep water away from tracks.

Santa Fe track-construction crews lay down tracks for the new Barstow Yard on January 6, 1975. Note the gauging rod straddling the rails, and the pairs of spikes neatly laid out on each tie. This track required ballasting, lining, tamping, and ballast-regulating before it was ready for service. William D. Middleton

Since both trains and weather are greatly damaging to track structure, maintenance workers must be vigilant in their inspection and maintenance of tracks to standards determined by the Federal Railroad Administration. These prescribed standards are based on the speed and level of traffic that track structures are intended to accommodate, the weight and speed of trains, and how heavily the tracks were constructed. Tracks designed to handle a constant parade of very heavy unit coal trains traveling at maximum track speed require far more intensive maintenance than lightly used storage tracks in a yard. The former may require inspection and maintenance on a daily basis, while the latter could function satisfactorily with minimal maintenance for decades. Heavily traveled lines require the heaviest rail with closely spaced ties and deep, well-manicured ballast. They need routine inspection, maintenance, and frequent replacement—especially on sharp curves. By contrast, on lightly used sidings and storage tracks, it is not unusual to find rail that dates from the steam era.

Traditionally, routine track maintenance was performed by locally based crews known as section gangs and assigned to specific sections of line, perhaps 10 to 20 miles in length. Under the authority of section foremen, these gangs maintained tracks on a day-to-day basis. They changed out worn rail sections, replaced damaged ties, and lined, surfaced, gauged, and tamped tracks. Among their important duties was also the maintenance of drainage ditches and culverts, which was a crucial task for ensuring good track conditions.

In areas affected by winter weather, section gangs assisted in clearing snow and ice from the line. It is important to clear snow from switches, especially the points and frogs—snow that isn't cleared as soon as it falls quickly turns to ice. Not only is ice more difficult to remove, but it is more likely to interfere with the function of switches, which can hamper operations and may result in a derailment. Likewise, level crossings with other lines need special attention, as do grade crossings with highways. If flangeways become clogged with ice, wheels can ride up and cause a derailment.

Rio Grande crews dump sand from gondolas on the narrow gauge on August 29, 1967. Hatches at the bottoms of the cars direct the flow of sand. John Gruber

A Milwaukee Road plow crew digs to free the railroad from snowdrifts on January 27, 1978. The night before, the train got stuck in a cut near DeForest, Wisconsin. The crews worked all day and into the cold night to clean out the heavy snow, pull the equipment from the drift, and get the railroad back in service. John Gruber

INSPECTION

Tracks must be inspected routinely by expert eyes looking for imperfections, damage, and wear. A track foreman, track inspector, or other qualified employee examines tracks and rights-of-way. Traditionally, this job was done by walking the line, but today inspections are often made from a Hyrail truck. However, it is still necessary to make close inspections on foot in high-traffic areas and known weak spots.

Switches require detailed inspection. Their complexity and moving points make them more susceptible to damage and more likely to cause derailments. Points must be examined for chips and wear, and the switch must be thrown to ensure the points are flush with no gaps that could result in wheel flanges taking the wrong course.

The switch frog is located at the junction of running rails and is designed to allow the wheel flange to pass from one set of rails to the other. Frogs take a constant battering from wheel flanges, and incur more wear than other track components. There are several varieties of frogs. One type requires guardrails that are opposite it to ensure that wheels are pulled to the desired side of the switch. Another type is a self-guarded frog that uses a raised area to ensure wheels take

Track foreman Albert Mallory oils switch points near the north end of Troy Station on the Troy Union Railroad in June 1950. He carries a large wicker broom and an oil can with a long-neck spout for directing the flow of oil. The signal tower that straddles the tracks in the distance controls switch points and signals using the mechanical pipeline that runs alongside the track. Jim Shaughnessy

🎧 A three-man HyRail crew on the Santa Fe sets down pilot wheels at a grade crossing at Edelstein, Illinois, in June 1984. Steve Smedley

the desired course. It is important to ensure that raised areas of self-guarded frogs do not suffer unusual wear.

Likewise, it is crucial that all areas of a switch remain within proper gauge parameters. In addition to checking the width between the running rails, workers must monitor the distance from the point of the frog to the guardrail. If this distance is out of gauge and goes uncorrected, the wheel flange may grab the wrong side of the frog point and cause the wheels to split the switch, which will result in derailment. In addition, the bolts that hold points and other crucial components need to be examined to ensure they are neither broken nor loose. The pounding of hundreds of wheels loosens components.

Like switches, level crossings with other tracks—commonly described as diamond crossings—are high-wear points that require close scrutiny and regular maintenance. Imagine the effects of a long freight train pounding across a diamond. Each car has eight wheels. Add another dozen wheels for each locomotive (assuming standard six-motor diesels are used). A typical coal train might carry 125 cars and require three big diesels—that means 1,036 heavy impacts on the crossing from just one train. On a busy line with dozens of heavy trains daily, it's no wonder that crossings are regularly inspected and routinely maintained.

Along the line, inspectors watch for defects and changes in the track structure. While the most serious flaws such as cracked and broken rails demand immediate repair, not every defect is as pressing. Although dangerous problems require the line to be closed and repairs must be made before the track can be used again, more commonly a track inspector simply downgrades track by imposing a speed restriction that allows continued passage of trains without the need for immediate repair. Some of these "slow orders" are permanent restrictions in places where trains must always move at slower-than-line speeds in order to operate safely. Slow orders imposed because of deteriorated track conditions are temporary slow orders. The length of time a temporary order is in place is determined by the individual railroad.

Slow orders may be imposed to compensate for a variety of defects. Inadequate drainage quickly damages track structure, as every passing train acts as a pump forcing more water up through the track bed. With that water comes silt and sludge that further clogs the ballast, soils the ties, and results in further deterioration. A track inspector may note drainage conditions that require attention, but are not causing an immediate problem. In a dry season, a blocked culvert is not dangerous. If it is not repaired, it may result in a washout during rainfall. Running water quickly destroys tracks. Following a cloudburst, a normally dry creek bed can become a raging destructive force. In minutes it can reduce a perfectly solid right-of-way into little more than rails hanging in the air.

The Federal Railroad Administration determines the factors that govern maximum track speed. One criterion is the number of good ties per 39 feet of track. The slowest acceptable grade of track for regular operation is known as Class I track, which requires a minimum of five good ties per 39 feet on tangent track. This figure allows freight trains to run at a maximum of 10 mph, and passenger trains at 15 mph. Although that speed is too slow for most running lines, it may be sufficient for yard or terminal trackage. When a railroad deems this speed fast enough, it does not need to spend more on maintenance than what's required to maintain tracks to this standard. By contrast, many heavy main lines are maintained to Class IV standards. These standards require a minimum of 12 good ties per 39 feet on tangent sections and 14 ties per 39 feet in curves sharper than 2 degrees. Then a 60-mph maximum is allowed for freight, and 80-mph maximum is allowed for passenger trains.

Despite its rough-looking appearance, a tie may be functioning as intended. Among other things, it needs to hold spikes (or other fasteners) in place to keep the rails in gauge. The condition of ties at rail joints is especially important. With Class I and II track, good ties support the track within 24 inches of the joint. With higher grades of track, requirements are even more stringent.

In addition to routine inspections, most main line railroads now use various types of mobile detection equipment. These tools help make periodic surveys and inspections to examine and document track structure, check rail condition, look for serious defects, and measure gauge. Some specialized inspections are contracted to firms such as Sperry, which has been in the business of performing detailed rail examinations since the 1920s. Traditionally, Sperry operated a fleet of specially equipped railcars. The railcars are now augmented by a growing fleet of specially designed Hyrail trucks; the trucks use induction and ultrasonic systems to detect transverse fissures and other rail flaws that cannot be found with visual inspections.

SECTION WORK

Traditionally, sections gangs used simple tools and muscle to repair tracks and rights-of-way. Tie replacement was a common job. Ballast was stripped back, spikes and tie plates were removed, tracks were raised with hand jacks, and long iron rods and tie tongs were employed to leverage the offending tie loose and pull it out of place. A new tie was inserted using the same tools. Heavy mauls were then used to spike rails to the new tie. E. E. Russell Tratman described correct spiking procedure in his 1901 book *Railway Track and Track Work*:

> Spiking should be done carefully, each spike being set vertically and driven straight down with its shank touching the edge of the rail base. The spiker should bring the maul down with a long swinging stroke, striking squarely on the head of the spike, and keeping his hands well down so that the handle of the maul will be approximately horizontal. He should in no case set the spike sloping from or towards him, as it reduces the hold of the spike head on the rail, while the spike may very likely be broken by the last blow of the maul and the spike will be bent by being pulled out.

Regularly tamping track is necessary to maintain a good track surface by ensuring that ballast evenly supports ties and the rails above. Tamping is often performed in conjunction with lining and surfacing work. Lining is the lateral adjustment of rails to remove kinks on tangent track and irregularities on curved track. Surfacing puts track on an even plane. Russell explained how tamping was traditionally accomplished:

> Tamping picks are used for stone, slag, or coarse clean gravel; tamping bars are used for earth, cinders, and ordinary gravel. In tamping with bars there should be an equal number of men on each side of the tie, standing opposite one another and striking in unison, so as to pack the material fairly and not drive it out at the opposite side of the tie. . . . The most thorough tamping should be directly under and for about 12 to 18 [inches] on each side of the rail, and tamping from ends will assist in getting a good firm bearing under the rail. Each tie should be fully and properly tamped before the men

leave it. On old track, the middle of the tie should not be tamped too hard, or the track will have a tendency to rock laterally, and the ties may be broken. When the track has once become center-bound in this way it is difficult to effect a remedy without disturbing the entire track, involving considerable work and expense.

Center-bound ties can often be identified by cracks in the middle. Severely bound ties will break. In this condition, they are of little use in either supporting rail or maintaining the gauge.

Continued on page 150

Foreman Gary Cooley takes a rail measurement during a rail-replacement procedure performed by a Wisconsin & Southern track gang at Madison, Wisconsin, in July 2005. Brian Solomon

145

Wisconsin & Southern track workers remove bolts from a
rail in preparation for rail replacement at the Madison
Yard. Brian Solomon

A California Northern track worker uses a crowbar to remove spikes from damaged track at Westley, California, along the former Southern Pacific West Side Line in July 2005. Brian Solomon

A California Northern track worker prepares rails for removal and replacement. Brian Solomon

Three California Northern track workers carry blue flags and other equipment back to their truck after finishing work for the day. Brian Solomon

A pair of California Northern track workers removes spikes in preparation for replacing rail. Brian Solomon

Continued from page 145

INCREASED PRODUCTIVITY

The labor-intensive nature of track maintenance made it among the earliest aspects of the railroad to benefit from mechanization. As early as 1900, steam-powered ditching equipment was common and experimental mechanical tamping machines were on offer. In addition, mechanized transport devices helped maintenance gangs get into position along the line. The first such vehicles were velocipedes and hand-pumped track cars, followed by small motor cars with gasoline engines. The most common motor cars were manufactured by Fairmont.

While local section gangs were normally responsible for replacing individual rail sections as the result of damage or specific rail-segment failure, specialized crews called steel gangs were organized to replace rail on longer line sections. Joseph A. Noble, who worked for Santa Fe, explained in his book, *From Cab to Caboose*:

> *At varying intervals, depending on the circumstances, the rail in a main track has to be renewed. This work is done by a "steel gang." The operation in general consists of pulling the spikes, throwing out the old rail and tie plates, adzing the ties to give a good bearing to the new tie plates, setting in the new rail, coupling it up, and spiking it. I have omitted some details of the work, but this is the essential procedure.*
>
> *Prior to 1925, we did all of this work by hand, including handling the rail, and with a gang of about 110 men, figured on averaging at least a track mile, this is the equivalent of a mile of rail on both sides re-laid, in a ten-hour day. As a rule, we laid one side all and brought the other side up the next day.*

Later Nobel, related:

> *In 1925 we got our first power equipment for laying rail, two air-operated spike drivers. Ordinarily, when laying rail by hand, the most time-consuming detail was the spiking, especially if you were laying around curves where there were hardwood ties. It was common practice, when the gang stopped laying to let a train by, to send men who could handle a spike maul back to help the spikers. Trains could be let over the newly laid rail at reduced speed before all the ties were spiked.*

Since the time period Nobel relates, machinery has been developed to perform almost every aspect of track maintenance, which has greatly reduced the amount of physical labor required for heavy track work. For example, automatic tie extractors and inserters allow ties to be replaced as fast as seven per minute. A modern-day steel gang uses an army of self-propelled machines. Other types of specialized roving gangs now perform much of the maintenance on large railroads. A tie gang replaces rotting ties with new ones, while a surfacing gang comes through with tampers and ballast regulators to line, surface, and gauge tracks. Depending on the type of work required, a railroad

↻ A member of a Burlington Northern Santa Fe steel gang prepares to lift a section of welded rail over to the track center. This rail section will be used to replace worn rail on the inside of a curve near Pepin, Wisconsin. *Brian Solomon*

↻ A Burlington Northern Santa Fe track worker helps place a guiding device on a section of welded rail so that a crane can lift it and slew it in place at Pepin, Wisconsin. *Brian Solomon*

🔊 A track gang lays new track west of English, Kentucky, on July 25, 1996. Bradley McClelland

🔊 This photo shows a Burlington Northern Santa Fe steel gang near Pepin, Wisconsin. Brian Solomon

may often combine rail-replacement, tie-replacement, and surfacing work. In much of the country, this work is typically performed seasonally. In temperate regions, the work is done from the end of spring until autumn, before the first frosts make such work difficult. By contrast, lines in warmer regions may aim to do heavy work before it gets prohibitively hot. While larger railroads now perform most track maintenance using machines, some short lines still rely on traditional methods and use track gangs to perform basic maintenance manually.

Traditionally, it was the responsibility of track crews to stay out of the way of trains. They could access tracks between scheduled and extra runs. Flagmen were stationed at the ends of work zones to protect workers and keep trains from entering sections under repair. Occasional errors in judgment could have dire consequences. Today's track crews on main lines are usually protected by the dispatcher, who issues written authority for them to work on specific sections of track. In yards, a yardmaster grants authority.

GLOSSARY

Absolute Permissive Block (APB): A system of automatic block signaling invented in 1911 that uses **permissive signals** for following moves but **absolute signals** for opposing moves, which facilitates the flow of traffic without compromising safety.

absolute signal: A fixed signal that must not be passed when displaying a "stop" **aspect**. A **home signal** is often also an absolute signal.

air brake: *See* **automatic air brake**.

air-brake schedule: The style and arrangement of air-brake handles and valves in the locomotive cab. Typical air-brake schedules include 6BL, 24RL, and 26L arrangements.

Amtrak: The working name of the National Railroad Passenger Corporation, the United States' national provider of intercity rail-passenger services. Amtrak was created in 1971 by an act of Congress to relieve privately owned railroads from the obligation of providing passenger service. Amtrak serves a political function while providing a desperately needed alternative to highway transport.

angle cock: A valve located at the ends of cars and locomotives used to open and close airflow through the **brake pipe**.

approach aspect: A cautionary **aspect** often used to slow **trains** that are approaching a **home signal** displaying a "stop" aspect. In most modern rulebooks, an approach aspect is indicated with a yellow signal light or a semaphore in a 45-degree diagonal position.

aspect: The information displayed by signal hardware. An aspect conveys an **indication** that has a specific meaning in accordance with a railway's rules.

automatic air brake: A braking system developed by George Westinghouse that uses stored compressed air as a control mechanism for both setting and releasing brakes. An air pump on the locomotive supplies compressed air for main air reservoirs that are used to charge the **brake pipe** that runs from car to car. The **brake pipe** conveys the air to reservoirs on each car. The system is designed to "fail safe" and any sudden loss in air pressure automatically applies the brakes. *See* **emergency brake application**.

automatic block signal: A **block signal** part of an **automatic block signal system** (ABS), actuated by track circuit and designed to reflect track condition and **block** occupancy. It may be combined with an interlocking network.

automatic block signal system: A network of defined **blocks** controlled by track circuit and governed by **automatic block signals** and/or **cab signals**.

block: 1. A length of track between clearly defined limits used to separate **trains**. Occupancy may be governed by fixed signals of either manual or automatic varieties, **cab signal**, staff, token, or written or verbal orders as prescribed by the rules of the railway operating the line. **2.** A group of freight cars organized at a yard for transit together to a common destination.

block system: A network of consecutive blocks used to separate **trains** by distance.

brake pipe: The air line that runs the length of a **train** to both deliver air to reservoirs on the cars and apply and release the **automatic air brakes** through controlled changes in air pressure.

cab signal: A system that displays signal **aspects** in the cab of a locomotive. It may be used in conjunction with fixed wayside signals or independent of them. It may also be combined with automatic **train** control.

Centralized Traffic Control (CTC): An interlocked remote control system that allows an operator/dispatcher to direct **train** movements over a railway line by signal indication. Typically, it gives the operator control of **switches**, signals, and other operating devices.

cornfield meet: The catastrophic result of misread or overlapping operating authority.

crew change: A location where crews are exchanged on long runs. Traditionally, crew districts were roughly 100 miles in length. During the 1970s and 1980s, crew districts were lengthened to improve productivity and now often measure several hundred miles in length.

crossover: An arrangement of **switches** designed to allow **trains** to cross from one main track to another.

CSX: One of the largest freight railroads operating in the eastern United States, CSX was created in 1980 through the merger of Chessie System and Seaboard Coast Line Industries. Although the initials are not an acronym, the name infers a company of its components multiplied.

direct traffic control (DTC): A system used for dispatching **trains** by radio that uses fixed **blocks**.

double track: Two main line tracks arranged for directional running by signal **indication** in the current of traffic as prescribed by Rule 251. Distinct from **two main track (TMT)**.

drawbar: A portion of the draft gear used to connect locomotives or railroad cars. May be used with or without a coupler, depending on the specific equipment arrangement.

dynamic brakes: System that uses reversing traction-motor current to function as electric generators that retard forward progress and allow the motors to work as brakes. Current is directed into air-cooled grids to dissipate generated energy. For the brakes to work, the engine must be running to turn the main generator and provide field excitation to the motors. The engineer needs to monitor the ammeter to avoid overloading motors, which can cause long-term damage.

emergency brake application: The controlled maximum application of the **automatic air brake**. In order to set the brakes rapidly in an emergency situation, a large porthole in the control mechanism is used to release **brake pipe** pressure as quickly as possible. An emergency application may be initiated intentionally by the engineer or accidentally through an unplanned interruption in the **brake pipe**, such as a separation of hoses between cars or a faulty brake valve. The action of making an emergency application has a variety of slang terms, including "dumping the air" and "the big hole."

flashover: A serious short circuit in the main generator or **traction motor**. It tends to occur in **traction motor**s at higher speeds when current fails to follow the normal desired path and can be very destructive to electrical equipment.

following movement: The movement of a **train** following another over the same section of track in the same direction. The opposite of an **opposing movement**.

frog: The part of a **switch** or crossing that permits wheel flanges to cross rails at an angle.

gear ratio: A locomotive **traction motor** uses a pinion gear to engauge a bull gear on the axle. Since the motor's maximum rotational speed is limited to avoid damage, reduction gearing is used to provide the desired speed-to-power relationship. A common gear ratio on Electro-Motive freight diesels is 62:15, where 62 refers to the number of teeth on the bull gear, and 15 is the teeth on the pinion gear. Locomotives with this ratio have a top recommended speed of 65 mph.

grade crossing: Where a highway crosses railroad tracks at grade—the bane and dread of every locomotive engineer.

grade-crossing protection: Signals that warn motorists to stop at **grade crossing**s.

ground relay: A protective device on a diesel-electric locomotive designed to prevent damage to electrical equipment in the event of a short circuit.

head end: The front of a **train**, including locomotive(s).

head-end crew: Members of the operating crew based on the locomotive, traditionally consisting of an engineer, fireman, and brakeman.

helper: A manned locomotive assigned to assist heavy **trains** in graded territory. Depending on the nature of operations and **train** make-up, helpers can operate at the **head end**, **rear end**, or middle of a **train**. On lines where helpers are routinely assigned to the back of **trains**, they are sometimes known as **pusher**s.

home signal: A fixed signal governing the entrance to a **block**, **interlocking plant**, or controlled point. In many situations, this is an **absolute signal** under control of a tower or dispatcher and thus must not be passed when displaying a "stop" **indication**. It is typically preceded by a distant signal.

hot box: A dangerous condition that occurs when there is a loss of lubricant in the axle-journal bearing, causing it to overheat and presenting the risk that the wheel may come loose from the axle, or that the axle itself may weaken and break in two.

hot-box detector: Trackside safety equipment designed to detect the presence of hot boxes in passing **trains**. Traditional hot-box detectors reported information to a signal tower or dispatching office, while modern hot-box detectors report automatically over the road channel of the **train** radio to issue an urgent audio warning to passing trains with specific information about affected axles.

independent: *See* **independent air brake**

independent air brake: A locomotive brake using an air-brake system that is entirely independent of the train air brake.

indication: The information given by a signal **aspect**.

industrial track: An auxiliary track used for switching or car storage. An industrial track is not used for normal running and may not be under control of a **block** system. Movements over such tracks are usually made at restricted speeds.

interlocking plant: A network of **switch**es, signals, and locks mechanically or electrically interconnected to ensure a predetermined order that prevents the arrangement of conflicting and opposing movements through said network.

interlocking signal: A signal controlled through mechanical or electrical means and interconnected with related **switch**es and signals to prevent the arrangement of conflicting and opposing movements through an **interlocking plant**. Normally such signals are absolute and cannot be passed when displaying a "stop" **indication**.

junction: A place where tracks come together. Normally used to describe the merging or crossing of two or more routes.

less-than-carload traffic (LCL): Small shipments that occupy less than a single freight car.

main generator: Turned by the prime mover on a diesel-electric locomotive, generates current to power the traction motors. More advance locomotives have an alternator rather than a main generator.

main line: A primary artery of a railroad that may consist of one or more **main track**s.

main track: A track designated for running.

mallet: A variety of compound steam locomotive that placed two engines under a common boiler. One engine used high-pressure steam directly from the boiler, which then exhausted at lower pressure to the other engine, and all is controlled by one engineer. Developed in Europe, the type was first used in the United States in 1904. The American application was intended to improve fuel efficiency and individual crew productivity. Pronounced *mal-lay*.

marker: A lamp or flag used to mark the **rear end** of a **train**. As defined by railroad rules, a **train** is incomplete unless a marker is displayed.

NORAC: Northeast Operation Rules Advisory Committee. A set of modern railroad operating rules that has been adopted by many railroads and commuter rail agencies operating in the northeastern United States.

on the ground: Railroad slang for a derailment, usually a minor one.

opposing movement: The movement of a train in the opposite direction of another train. The opposite of a **following movement**.

permissive aspect: An aspect displayed by a manual **block** signal that permits movement at restricted speed into an occupied **block**.

permissive signal: A fixed signal, usually in **automatic block signal** territory, that displays "stop and proceed," or in some situations "restricting," as its most restrictive **aspect**s. Such signals are clearly distinguished from absolute signals, usually by number plates or letter markings.

points: The movable part of a **switch** used to direct wheel flanges from one set of tracks to another. In the British lexicon, the term is used to describe the whole switch.

pusher: *See* **helper**.

rear end: The back of the train, traditionally punctuated by a caboose displaying **marker** lamps, is now indicated by a telemetry device or red flag.

restricted speed: A slow speed defined by railroad rules. The actual speed varies between different **rulebook**s. **NORAC** defines movement at restricted speed under Rule 80 which states,
Movement at Restricted Speed must apply the following three requirements as the method of operation:
  1) Control the movement to permit stopping within one half the range of vision short of;
    a) Other trains or railroad equipment occupying or fouling the track,
    b) Obstructions,
    c) Switches not properly lined for movement,
    d) Derails set in the derailing position,
    e) Any signal requiring a stop.
AND
  2) Look out for broken or mis-aligned track.
AND
  3) Do not exceed 20 mph outside interlocking limits and 15 mph within interlocking limits. This restriction applies to the entire movement, unless otherwise specified in the rule or instruction that requires Restricted Speed.

restricting aspect: A signal **aspect** that authorizes a train to travel at **restricted speed**. Railroad slang refers to it as a "know nothing" signal because beyond the point at which the signal is displayed, you "know nothing" about track condition or occupancy. If you hit anything, however, you "own" it.

rulebook: A detailed list of rules for use by railway employees that defines the method of conduct regarding railway operations.

rules violation: An infraction of the company rules by an employee. Depending on the seriousness of the infraction, it may result in discipline or dismissal from service.

runaway train: A **train** without sufficient braking power to stop.

searchlight signal: A variety of color light that uses a single lamp and a focused beam. Sometimes called a "target signal" because of its shape.

section: 1. Under the old **timetable** and **train-order** rules, more than one **train** was allowed to operate on the authority granted in the **timetable**. When this occurred, each **train** was a section of the **timetable**-scheduled **train**. Green flags (or classification lamps) were displayed when more than one section was operated to alert other **trains** and employees that another section would follow. The last section was designated by the presence of white flags (or lamps). **2.** A portion of line designated such for maintenance purposes.

section gang: A maintenance gang in charge of routine track work on a **section** of line.

semaphore: A traditional signal that displays **aspect**s by the position of its arm or blade. It may be operated by manual, mechanical, pneumatic, or electrical means, and may be used in combination with colored lights.

set out: A railroad car (or a group of cars) in a **train** or on a track that has been designated to either be set apart from the train or that has already been set apart—that is, placed on a **siding**.

siding: A running track used for the meeting or passing of **train**s.

signal aspect: *See* **aspect**.

slip switch: An arrangement of tracks that combines a crossing and a **switch** using multiple sets of **point**s and **frog**s.

spring switch: A **switch** that is operated by hand, but which can accept trailing **train** movements in either position without risk of derailment. Springs automatically return the **point**s to their normal position.

spur: An auxiliary track that is not used for running, and which may be used to store cars, locomotives, or other equipment.

station: May include structures such as station buildings and other facilities, but is not necessarily a traditional structure. A station as defined by railroad rules is "a location identified by name in the timetable." Thus, it may be as little as a post in the ground with the name of the location painted on it. It may be a point with or without a **switch** or **siding**.

switch: A track arrangement consisting of rails, **point**s, and a **frog** that controls movement between tracks. Ordinary switches have two positions: normal and reverse. In railroad terminology, a switch may be "lined normal" or "lined reverse." If it has been in the reverse position and is moved back to the normal position, it has been "restored to normal."

switcher: A locomotive assigned to local or **yard** work sorting railroad cars.

switching: The organization of railroad cars by moving them from one track to another.

switchman: A brakeman's position on a **yard** crew. The term stems from the traditionally craft division between **yard** crews and road crews.

timetable: Printed schedules and special instructions regarding the movement of **train**s. Using the "timetable and **train order**" system of **train** control, an employee timetable (rather than the common variety issued for the convenience of passengers and shippers) authorized the movement of **train**s.

traction motor: The electric motor used on electric and diesel-electric locomotives to convert electrical energy to rotary motion.

tractive effort: A measure of the force of the locomotive to move a train.

train: An engine with or without cars, or multiple-unit passenger equipment. Traditionally an engine and cars had to display **marker** lamps or flags before being considered a train.

trainmaster: A supervisory position overseeing the assigning, scheduling, and day-to-day management of **train**s and **train** crews, including their discipline and grievances.

train order: A paper order issued by an authorized member of railway operating staff, often a train dispatcher, that gives clear and specific instructions regarding the operations of **train**s. Typically issued on a standard form, train orders may be used to modify, alter, or append operating instructions printed in an employee **timetable**.

two main track (TMT): A double-track arrangement whereby trains may operate in either direction on either track without regard to the current of traffic rules and typically controlled by **Centralized Traffic Control** or a similar arrangement.

unit: By one standard definition, a diesel-electric locomotive consists of all the locomotives connected together using multiple-unit technology; thus, each individual component of the locomotive is a unit. In most situations, these units may also function as individual locomotives. Locomotive units without control cabs are known as B units.

unit train: A train that carries one commodity—typically coal, grain, oil, or ore—from origin to final destination using a fixed consist of cars.

valve gear: On a steam engine, the arrangement of rods and eccentrics used to regulate steam admission and exhaust from the cylinder during the piston stroke.

wheel slip: The loss of adhesion between locomotive drive wheels and the rail. Momentary wheel slip results in lower **tractive effort**, which reduces the pulling power of a locomotive. Left unchecked, wheel slip can cause a **train** to stall.

yard: A network of tracks used for assembling **train**s and/or storing cars and other railroad equipment. Movement on yard tracks is generally unsignaled and limited to **restricted speed**.

yard limits: A section of line or tracks designated by yard limit signs where operations fall under distinctive rules designed to facilitate switching and related activities, as well as **main line** movements.

BIBLIOGRAPHY

BOOKS

Alymer-Small, Sidney. *The Art of Railroading, Vol. VIII.* Chicago, 1908.

American Railway Signaling Principles and Practices. New York, n.d.

Armstrong, John H. *The Railroad: What It Is, What It Does.* Omaha, Nebr., 1982.

Bean, W. L. *Twenty Years of Electrical Operation on the New York, New Haven and Hartford Railroad.* East Pittsburgh, Pa., 1927.

Brignano, Mary and Hax McCullough. *The Search for Safety: A History of Railroad Signals and the People Who Made Them.* Pittsburgh, Pa., 1981.

Churella, Albert J. *From Steam to Diesel.* Princeton, N.J., 1998.

Doherty, Timothy Scott and Brian Solomon. *Conrail.* St. Paul, Minn., 2004.

Droege, John A. *Freight Terminals and Trains.* New York, 1912.

Elements of Railway Signaling. Rochester, N.Y., 1979.

Farrington, S. Kip, Jr. *Railroading from the Head End.* New York, 1943.

———. *Railroading from the Rear End.* New York, 1946.

———. *Railroading the Modern Way.* New York, 1951.

———. *Railroads at War.* New York, 1944.

———. *Railroads of the Hour.* New York, 1958.

———. *Railroads of Today.* New York, 1949.

Frey, Robert L. *Railroads in the Nineteenth Century.* New York, 1988.

Garmany, John Bonds. *Southern Pacific Dieselization.* Edmonds, Wash., 1985.

General Electric. *New Series Diesel-Electric Locomotive Operating Manual.* Erie, Pa., 1979.

Holbrook, Stewart Hall. *Story of American Railroads.* New York, 1947.

Hungerford, Edward. *Daniel Willard Rides the Line.* New York, 1938.

Keilty, Edmund. *Interurbans Without Wires.* Glendale, Calif., 1979.

Kirkland, John F. *Dawn of the Diesel Age: The History of the Diesel Locomotive in America.* Pasadena, Calif., 1994.

———. *The Diesel Builders, Vols. I, II, and III.* Glendale, Calif., 1983.

Middleton, William D. *Grand Central: The World's Greatest Railway Terminal.* San Marino, Calif. 1977.

———. *Landmarks on the Iron Road: Two Centuries of North American Railroad Engineering.* Bloomington, Ind., 1999.

———. *When the Steam Railroads Electrified.* Milwaukee, Wis., 1974.

Noble, Joseph A. *From Cab to Caboose.* Norman, Okla., 1964.

Ransome-Wallis, P. *World Railway Locomotives.* New York, 1959.

Raymond, William G., revised by Henry E. Riggs and Walter C. Sadler. *The Elements of Railroad Engineering, 5th Ed.* New York, 1937.

Reck, Franklin M. *The Dilworth Story: The Biography of Richard Dilworth Pioneer Developer of the Diesel Locomotive.* New York, 1954.

Riddell, Doug. *From the Cab: Stories from a Locomotive Engineer.* Pasadena, Calif., 1999.

Salisbury, Stephen. *No Way to Run a Railroad: The Untold Story of the Penn Central Crisis.* New York, 1982.

Saunders, Richard, Jr. *Main Lines: American Railroads 1970–2002.* DeKalb, Ill., 2003.

———. *Merging Lines: American Railroads 1900–1970.* DeKalb, Ill., 2001.

———. *The Railroad Mergers and the Coming of Conrail.* Westport, Conn., 1978.

Shearer, Frederick E. *The Pacific Tourist: The 1884 Illustrated Trans-continental Guide of Travel from the Atlantic to the Pacific Ocean.* New York, 1970.

Signor, John R. *Southern Pacific–Santa Fe Tehachapi.* San Marino, Calif. 1983.

Solomon, Brian. *The American Diesel Locomotive.* Osceola, Wis., 2000.

———. *The American Steam Locomotive.* Osceola, Wis., 1998.

———. *GE Locomotives: 110 Years of General Electric Motive Power.* St. Paul, Minn., 2003.

———. *Locomotive.* St. Paul, Minn., 2001.

———. *Railroad Signaling.* St. Paul, Minn., 2003.

Staff, Virgil. *D-Day on the Western Pacific: A Railroad's Decision to Dieselize.* Glendale, Calif., 1982.

Stover, John F. *The Life and Decline of the American Railroad.* New York, 1970.

Swingle, Calvin F. *Standard Rules for Movement of Trains*. Chicago, 1908.

Thompson, Slason. *The Railway Library–1912*. Chicago, 1913.

———. *Short History of American Railways*. Chicago, 1925.

Thoms, William E. *Reprieve for the Iron Horse: The Amtrak Experiment—Its Predecessors and Prospects*. Baton Rouge, La., 1973

Tratman, E. E. Russell. *Railway Track and Track Work*. New York, 1901.

Trewman, H. F. *Electrification of Railways*. London, 1920.

Vance, Jr., James E. *The North American Railroad: Its Origin, Evolution, and Geography*. Baltimore, Md., 1995.

Wilner, Frank N. *The Amtrak Story*. Omaha, Nebr., 1994.

PERIODICALS

Jane's World Railways. London.

Official Guide to the Railways. New York.

Pacific RailNews. Waukesha, Wis. [No longer published.]

Passenger Train Journal. Waukesha, Wis. [No longer published.]

Railroad History (formerly *Railway and Locomotive Historical Society Bulletin*). Boston, Mass.

Railroad Magazine (now part of *Railfan & Railroad*). New York.

Railway Age. Chicago and New York.

Railway Gazette (1870–1908). New York. [No longer published.]

The Railway Gazette. London.

Railway Signaling and Communications (formerly *The Railway Signal Engineer*, nee *Railway Signaling*). Chicago and New York. [No longer published.]

Trains. Waukesha, Wis.

Vintage Rails. Waukesha, Wis. [No longer published.]

BROCHURES, TIMETABLES, AND RULEBOOKS

Atchison, Topeka & Santa Fe Railway. *Signal Training Vols. 1 & 2*. 1977.

Chicago Operating Rules Association. *Operating Guide*. [1994?].

General Code of Operating Rules, 4th Ed. 2000.

General Electric. *Dash 8 Locomotive Line*. n.d.

———. *GE Diesel Engines–Power for Progress*. Erie, Pa., 1988.

———. *A New Generation for Increased Productivity*. Erie, Pa., 1987.

———. *Series-7 diesel-electric locomotives*. Erie, Pa., 1980.

General Motors. *Electro-Motive Division Model F3 Operating Manual No. 2308B*. LaGrange, Ill., 1948.

———. *Electro-Motive Division Operating Manual No. 2300*. LaGrange, Ill., [1945?].

———. *Electro-Motive Division SDP40F Operator's Manual, 2nd Ed.* LaGrange, Ill., 1974.

Metro-North Railroad. *Rules of the Operating Department*. 1999.

———. *Timetable No. 1*. 2001.

New York Central System. *Rules for the Government of the Operating Department*. 1937.

NORAC Operating Rules, 7th Ed. 2000.

Seaboard Coast Line Railroad Co. *Instructions and Information Pertaining to Diesel Electric Engines*. Jacksonville, Fla., 1972.

———. *Train Handling Instruction and Information Pertaining to Air Brake Equipment on Engines and Cars*. Jacksonville, Fla., 1975.

INDEX

Amtrak, 12, 16, 24, 27, 86, 96, 130
Atlantic Coast Line, 32
Baltimore & Ohio, 31, 51, 63
Barkoviak, Mike, 111
Beecher, Marshall, 128
Belt Railway, 47, 132
Benjamine, Walt, 49
Berryman, R. T., 71
Berryman, Travis, 105, 106
Berwaldt, Jim, 94
Beyer family, 10
Binkley, Kent, 33
Bluebell Railway, 76
Bob, Brenda, 133
Boomer, 51
Boston & Albany, 60, 62
Boston & Maine, 17, 118, 125
Brakeman, 12, 16, 17, 20, 22, 36–51, 53, 55, 58, 60, 63, 84
    Head-end, 48–50
Brotherhood of Locomotive Engineers, 16
Brotherhood of Sleeping Car Porters, 13
Bruley, Jerold J., 11
Buffalo & Pittsburgh, 34
Burke, Tim, 12
Burkhardt, Ed, 74
Burlington Northern, 55, 67, 99, 111, 124
Burlington Northern Santa Fe, 52, 63, 69, 71, 73, 105, 106, 129, 136, 151, 153
Burlington Route, 31, 115
Burrington family, 8
Cain family, 8
California Northern, 66, 67, 103, 147–149
Campbell, John, 132
Canadian National, 11, 77, 87, 108, 118, 122
Canadian Pacific, 34, 76, 85, 116, 131
Capitol Limited, 123
Centralized Traffic Control, 19, 23, 28, 57, 125–127, 131, 132
Chapman, R. K., 42
Chesapeake & Ohio, 58, 63
Chicago & Alton, 12
Chicago & Milwaukee, 130, 131
Chicago & North Western, 8, 13, 41, 68, 72, 101, 105, 130
Chicago Metra, 128, 134
Chicago Regional Transit Authority, 8
City of Westfield, 100
Clark, Will, 15
Clerk, 55
Conductor, 34, 37, 39, 41, 42, 45, 47, 49, 52–73, 115, 128
Conrail, 60, 62, 63, 92, 111, 121, 122, 138
Cooley, Gary, 145
Cox, Alex, 8

Cruickshank, Greg, 60, 62
CSX, 42, 51, 58, 63, 123, 129
Cumbres & Toltec Scenic, 54
Cyprus Northshore Mining, 126
Dakota 400, 12
Davis, Martin, 90
Delaware & Hudson, 18, 49, 90, 113, 115
Delaware, Lackawanna & Western, 24, 34, 45, 68, 70, 102, 127
Dieselization, 28, 86, 88
Dispatchers, 116, 117, 128–137
Duffy, E. J., 61
Electrician, 27
Elgin, Joliet & Eastern, 130, 131
Emerson, Jim, 35
Empire State Express, 98
Engineer, 16, 20, 28, 34, 37, 40, 44, 53, 66, 69, 74–107
English, Frank, 14, 15
Erie Railroad, 24, 32, 114
Erie-Lackawanna, 61, 99
Farence, Tom, 8, 13
Federal Hours of Service Act, 91, 128
Federal Railroad Administration, 140, 144
Fireman, 48, 55, 58, 74–107
Flagman, 48
Fonda, R. P., 125
Fox Valley & Western, 11
Frackiewicz, Henry, 94
Freight conductor, 17
French, Mark, 66, 67
Frisco, 67
Garza, Paul. 136
Grand Central, 14
Green Bay & Western, 10, 11
Grumblatt, Jay, 121–123, 129
Gunter, John, 58
Hanson, Doug, 13
Haseltine, Ray, 76
Heller, Dave, 45, 47
Hiawatha, 10
Holbrook, Tim, 66, 67, 103
Holyoke & Westfield, 63
Humpmaster, 33
Hurt, Patricia, 96
Illinois Central, 135
Inspector, 142–144
Itel, 10
Jackson, Denny, 107
Janesko, Richard, 34
Janney, Eli H., 43
Joint Council of Dining Car Employees, 13
Josserand, Peter, 55
Kaneko, Sheldon, 63
Kansas City Southern, 107
King, Ed, 130, 131
King, Fred, 28
Kitchen, Henry, 91
Kopak, Dan, 122

Kowanski, George W., 76, 92–94, 96, 98
Lackawanna, 32
Larson, Don, 126
Laurentian, 113
Leverman, 109–137
Loften, Fred, 12
Logan, Wayne, 99
Machinist, 34
Maglione, Lenny, 15
Maine Central, 110, 116, 117
Malcewicz, Frank, 44
Mallory, Albert, 142
Manro, C. L., 65
Maryland Midland, 59
Massey, Al, 100
McCloud River Railroad, 105
McGee, H. Weldon, 10
McMaster, Dan, 59
Mechanic, 23
Metro-North, 15, 27, 61–63, 76, 93, 96, 120, 123, 129
Mild, Clarence, 134
Milwaukee Road, 8, 12, 91, 113, 124, 130, 131, 134, 141
Morrow, Jim, 49
Nelson, J., 71
New Haven, 15, 60, 62, 63, 89, 92, 121
New York Central, 15, 32, 39, 60, 62, 68, 98, 120–123, 125
New York, Ontario & Western, 23, 24
New York, Susquehanna & Western, 43
New York, West Shore & Buffalo, 60
Nichols, Roger, 15
Nickel Plate Road, 18, 20, 29, 85, 110
Nobel, Joseph A., 150, 151
North Coast Limited, 9, 41
North Shore line, 44
Northern Pacific, 25, 41, 51, 65
Olesnyckyj, Taras, 27
Operator, 55, 109–137
Palermo, Shawn, 34, 45, 68, 70, 127
Passenger conductor, 17
Penn Central, 60, 62, 92
Pennsylvania Railroad, 32, 51, 68, 84, 134
Photographer, 14, 15
Pierce, Mark, 106
Pioneer Valley Railroad, 62, 100
Pitarys, George S., 116, 117
Polus, Peter, 41
Pronschinske family, 10
Radio, 28, 57, 73
Railway Labor Executives Association, 13
Rhodes family, 8
Riddell, Doug, 48, 54, 68, 86, 87, 92, 96, 97, 99
Rio Grande, 39, 54, 89, 141

Rochester 400, 41
Rose, Dick, 33
Runyon, Larry, 63
Sage, Merle, 115
Santa Fe Railway, 42, 51, 63, 74, 95, 100, 107, 140, 143, 150
Scharf, Carl, 123
Scruggs, J. C., 115
Seaboard Air Line, 91
Seaboard Coast Line, 32, 68, 104
Section gangs, 145–149
Semple, Bill, 27
Sherman, Ken, 113
Shipley family, 8
Shopman, 25, 31
Shultz family, 10
Smith, Josh, 52
Sansalla family, 10, 11
South Eastern & Chatham Railway, 76
Southern Pacific, 19, 28, 33, 36, 51, 66, 67, 103, 111, 133, 136, 147
Southern Railway, 50
Spangler family, 12
Staggers Act, 32
Station agent, 27
Suddeth, Frank, 129
Superintendent, 16
Swanson, Paul, 91
Switchman, 42–45
Telegraph, 19, 20, 113
Telegraph operator, 16
Thigpen, Henry, 135
Time zones, 110, 111
Towers, 120–124
Trainmaster, 16
Troy Union Railroad, 142
Tutland Railroad, 76
Union Pacific, 33, 51, 57
Unions, 13, 16
United Parcel Service (UPS), 33, 106, 129
United States Railroad Administration (USRA), 12, 25
Vargo, Jim, 123
VIA Rail, 96
Volts, Steve, 73
Wall, Jim, 135
Western Maryland, 8
Western Pacific, 55, 125, 126
White, Frank, 65
Wisconsin & Southern, 12, 81, 101, 145, 146
Wisconsin Central Ltd., 11, 74, 108, 118
Worchester, Jerry, 106
Yampa Valley Mail, 89
Yancey, Rob, 86, 87
Yardmaster, 27, 33
Zephyr, 10